CAMBRIDGE LIBRARY COLLECTION

Books of enduring scholarly value

Travel and Exploration

The history of travel writing dates back to the Bible, Caesar, the Vikings and the Crusaders, and its many themes include war, trade, science and recreation. Explorers from Columbus to Cook charted lands not previously visited by Western travellers, and were followed by merchants, missionaries, and colonists, who wrote accounts of their experiences. The development of steam power in the nineteenth century provided opportunities for increasing numbers of 'ordinary' people to travel further, more economically, and more safely, and resulted in great enthusiasm for travel writing among the reading public. Works included in this series range from first-hand descriptions of previously unrecorded places, to literary accounts of the strange habits of foreigners, to examples of the burgeoning numbers of guidebooks produced to satisfy the needs of a new kind of traveller - the tourist.

History of the Two Tartar Conquerors of China

The publications of the Hakluyt Society (founded in 1846) made available edited (and sometimes translated) early accounts of exploration. The first series, which ran from 1847 to 1899, consists of 100 books containing published or previously unpublished works by authors from Christopher Columbus to Sir Francis Drake, and covering voyages to the New World, to China and Japan, to Russia and to Africa and India. This history of China derives from the writings of the Jesuit Ferdinand Verbiest (1623–88), who was sent as a missionary to China, and eventually, following a contest with the leading Chinese astronomer, became Head of the Mathematical Board and Director of the Beijing Observatory for the Kangxi Emperor. He became a trusted advisor to the emperor, learning the Manchu language so as to be able to instruct him in mathematics. He also improved the process of casting cannon, and adjusted the Chinese calendar, which had acquired an extra month through inaccurate astronomical calculations. The introduction to this edition, published in 1854, sketches the life of Verbiest and discusses the sources of the text; an appendix gives a description by Verbiest himself of a hunting expedition on which he accompanied the emperor.

Cambridge University Press has long been a pioneer in the reissuing of out-of-print titles from its own backlist, producing digital reprints of books that are still sought after by scholars and students but could not be reprinted economically using traditional technology. The Cambridge Library Collection extends this activity to a wider range of books which are still of importance to researchers and professionals, either for the source material they contain, or as landmarks in the history of their academic discipline.

Drawing from the world-renowned collections in the Cambridge University Library, and guided by the advice of experts in each subject area, Cambridge University Press is using state-of-the-art scanning machines in its own Printing House to capture the content of each book selected for inclusion. The files are processed to give a consistently clear, crisp image, and the books finished to the high quality standard for which the Press is recognised around the world. The latest print-on-demand technology ensures that the books will remain available indefinitely, and that orders for single or multiple copies can quickly be supplied.

The Cambridge Library Collection will bring back to life books of enduring scholarly value (including out-of-copyright works originally issued by other publishers) across a wide range of disciplines in the humanities and social sciences and in science and technology.

History of the Two Tartar Conquerors of China

Including the Two Journeys into Tartary of Father Ferdinand Verbiest, in the Suite of the Emperor Kanh-Hi

PIERRE JOSEPH D' ORLÉANS
NICHOLAAS WITSEN
EDITED BY RICHARD HENRY MAJOR

CAMBRIDGE
UNIVERSITY PRESS

CAMBRIDGE UNIVERSITY PRESS

Cambridge, New York, Melbourne, Madrid, Cape Town, Singapore,
São Paolo, Delhi, Dubai, Tokyo, Mexico City

Published in the United States of America by Cambridge University Press, New York

www.cambridge.org
Information on this title: www.cambridge.org/9781108008129

This edition first published 1854
This digitally printed version 2010

ISBN 978-1-108-00812-9 Paperback

WORKS ISSUED BY

The Hakluyt Society.

HISTORY OF THE TWO TARTAR

CONQUERORS OF CHINA.

M.DCCC.LIV.

HISTORY

OF THE TWO

TARTAR CONQUERORS

OF

CHINA,

INCLUDING THE TWO JOURNEYS INTO TARTARY OF FATHER FERDINAND
VERBIEST, IN THE SUITE OF THE EMPEROR KANG-HI:

From the French of

PÈRE PIERRE JOSEPH D'ORLÉANS,

OF THE COMPANY OF JESUS.

TO WHICH IS ADDED FATHER PEREIRA'S JOURNEY INTO TARTARY IN THE
SUITE OF THE SAME EMPEROR,

From the Dutch of

NICOLAAS WITSEN.

TRANSLATED AND EDITED BY

THE EARL OF ELLESMERE.

With an Introduction

BY

R. H. MAJOR, ESQ.,

OF THE BRITISH MUSEUM,
HONORARY SECRETARY OF THE HAKLUYT SOCIETY.

LONDON:

PRINTED FOR THE HAKLUYT SOCIETY.

M.DCCC.LIV.

THE HAKLUYT SOCIETY.

INTRODUCTION.

THERE are two reasons why the selection of the present work for translation and publication by the
Hakluyt Society, has been considered peculiarly ap-
propriate and desirable. The one that, though bearing a title of a purely historical character, it embodies
the observations of various missionaries in China, together with the highly interesting narratives of two
journeys into Tartary in the years 1682 and 1683,
made by the famous Jesuit father Ferdinand Verbiest,
in the suite of the Chinese emperor. The other, that
at a time like the present, when a revolution of the
most formidable character has rendered the maintenance of the throne of China by the existing Tartar
dynasty a matter of great uncertainty, the translation
of a scarce work, by an author of celebrity, describing
the establishment of that dynasty, seemed to have an
especial claim upon the reader's interest and attention.

As regards the former, and for the general pur-
poses of the Hakluyt Society the more important of
these two considerations, the period brought under
our notice by the event treated of, is also one
of remarkably prominent interest in the history of

European missions amongst the Chinese, a people to whom the "penitus toto divisos orbe" of Virgil might for many reasons so well be applied. In the introduction to Mendoza, edited for the Hakluyt Society by Sir George Staunton, the present writer has already given an account of the numerous painful and perilous attempts which had been made by Europeans, to establish themselves in this exclusive country, up to the close of the sixteenth century. The last effort there alluded to, and the first which was really successful, was that made by the distinguished Jesuit Matteo Ricci, who, in the year 1600, not only contrived to gain access to the emperor in Pekin, but in the following year had a house assigned to him, and was taken into the emperor's service. To him, in fact, may justly be attributed the foundation of the Catholic mission. Once established at Pekin, no difficulties dismayed him; and to his zealous perseverance was added an extent of scientific knowledge, exactly coincident with the tastes of the Chinese, which, as a means towards success, was truly invaluable. His prudence in conciliating the prejudices of the Chinese, which by many has been stigmatized as a dereliction of principle, aided greatly in furthering his objects, and he gained both friends and converts in considerable numbers. Other Jesuits attached themselves to the mission, and settled themselves at various stations between the capital and Canton, and too much praise cannot be given to the zeal and intelligence with which these devoted men followed up the noble cause which they had undertaken. Indeed,

so successful were their efforts, that as Sir John Davis
has observed, in his valuable work on " The Chinese,"
" Had it not been for the narrow-minded bigotry and
intolerance with which some of the popes, and the
monks whom they deputed to China, frustrated the
labours of the more sober-minded Jesuits, Europeans
and their religion might at this day enjoy a very different footing in the empire." Ricci died in 1610,
but during the reign of the emperor Wan-lëĕ, the
mission continued to be regarded with favour by the
court until the year 1615, when through the jealousy
of the Bonzes, a persecution was raised against the
Christians, which resulted in stripes and imprisonment
to many of them, and the expulsion to Macao of those
who were in the neighbourhood of the court. Alvaro
Semedo, who, in his " Imperio de la China," has given
an account of this persecution, himself only escaped
the bastinado in consideration of a severe illness under
which he was labouring. To this change in the conduct of the emperor Wan-lëĕ, the author of the present volume, in his religious zeal, attributes as a
retributive consequence the commencement of that
revolution which not very long afterwards wrested
the throne of China from the native or Ming dynasty.

It was in 1618, two years before the death of
Wan-lëĕ, that Tien-ming, a chieftain of the Manchu
Tartars, and lineal ancestor of the present emperor,
published a manifesto containing seven subjects of
grievance which he proclaimed himself called upon to
revenge. The fierce inroads of this daring warrior,
who had already assumed the title of emperor, though

not successful in securing the capital city of Pekin, were yet most formidable in their effects upon the stability of the throne. Numerous bodies of rebels, taking example from the boldness of the attempt, arose within the country itself, and thus exposed it to a more easy conquest by the common invader. Repulsed from the capital, which he had prepared to besiege, Tien-ming retired into the province of Leaotung, which he harassed with the most unsparing cruelties. Various success attended the progress of these political struggles for several years. Meanwhile the missionaries fared but ill, being exposed to frequent painful acts of persecution, though happily the edict of expulsion from the country was not absolutely carried into effect. The death of Wan-lëĕ occurred in 1620, but it was not till 1622 that a reversal of the edict of expulsion of the missionaries was obtained, and a cessation of the persecution of so many years effected. This was brought about by the instrumentality of a native Christian, a mandarin of great talent and influence, whose Chinese name was Siu, but who at his baptism had received the name of Paul. His conversion had been effected by the arguments of Ricci, to whose prosperity, as well as that of the church at large, he had been able by his abilities, position, and zealous ardour in the Christian cause, to contribute most essentially. To him and his daughter Candida that cause was already indebted for the erection of thirty-nine churches in various provinces, and the printing of a hundred and thirty Christian works in Chinese, for the instruction of the people.

In the above-mentioned year 1622, arrived in China the celebrated Jesuit, Adam Schaal, or Schall, whose skill in mathematics and the experimental sciences constituted him a fitting successor to the illustrious Ricci. He was a German by birth, having beên born at Cologne in 1591. His talents and learning, employed for several years with great success in the province of Shen-si, introduced him at length to the notice of Paul, who, in the year 1628, recommended him warmly to the regard of the emperor, and he became a great favourite at court. Among the Chinese, the science of astronomy seemed to be the very passport of the missionary. To this study Schall, therefore, devoted assiduous attention; and by this means engaged for himself so much goodwill among the people, that not only the newly made converts, but those who were unconverted also, willingly lent him a helping hand in the construction of a Christian church. During the long series of political troubles which brought about the subversion of the Ming dynasty, and the establishment of the present race upon the throne of China, as recounted in the volume before us, Adam Schall retained his high position at the court of Pekin. Nor was this influence diminished by the changes in the imperial house. In 1634, in conjunction with Father Giacomo Rho (in whose company, as well as that of the well known Nicolas Trigault, to whom we owe so much of our knowledge respecting China at that period, he had made the journey to China), he was charged with the responsible task of revising the imperial calendar. Father Rho dying in 1638, this duty rested solely with Schall, who was engaged upon it during three consecutive reigns, viz., that of the last sovereign of the Ming dynasty, and those of the two first Tartar Chinese emperors. Meanwhile, however, although the Manchu rebels had gained the mastery in the north of China, the south had not yet bowed to the Tartar yoke. In that portion of the empire some members of the old imperial family of the Ming were converted to Christianity, and their cause was consequently favoured by the missionaries in that region. Two Christian Chinese generals made head against the Tartar army, and with success; and Yunlié, the claimant to the throne, was in consequence proclaimed emperor. His mother, wife, and son, were baptised with the names of Helena, Maria, and Constantine. Helena, to manifest her attachment to the cause of Christianity, despatched a letter to Pope Alexander VIII, by the hands of Michael Boym, a Polish Jesuit, in which she expressed her desire to place the country, through him, under the protection of God. All hope, however, from such a source was soon put to an end, for in that same year 1651 Chunchi, the youthful heir of the late Tartar conqueror, being declared of age, assumed the reins of government at Pekin; and the Tartars, impatient of completing their conquest, made a desperate attack upon the southern provinces. Yunlié was vanquished, and both he and his youthful son perished. Helena was led captive to Pekin, and the imperial race of the Ming became extinct. Under the emperor Chunchi, Schall still remained in the same favoured position at the court of Pekin, as he had done under the previous sovereigns. The Tartar monarch appointed him President of the Astronomical Board, and conferred upon him various marks of his regard and approbation. During the reign of this emperor, the prosperity of the Jesuit missions at the court was very great; many churches were built and converts made, while fresh accessions of labourers were admitted into the country. Among these the most important, and one who holds a prominent part in the narrative now before us, was the Father Ferdinand Verbiest, a German Jesuit, who arrived in China in 1659, and became the coadjutor of Schall in presiding over the tribunal of mathematics. During the whole of the reign of Chunchi the cause of Christianity prospered in the kingdom of China, but the close of his life did not justify the hopes of conversion which his conduct during his earlier years had given rise to. The influence of the Bonzes over him through the latter part of his reign became complete. Upon his death in 1661, the government, during the minority of Kanghi, fell into the hands of four regents, whose known opposition to the new sect led to the sending in of a memorial to the court, in which the mischiefs which might ensue from a continuance of the prosperity of the Christians were fully dwelt upon. The dissensions which had arisen between the Jesuits and the Dominicans, with every other argument which could put the motives of the Christians in an unfavourable light, were therein adduced with all the earnestness of antagonism. This injurious memorial had its desired effect, and a fear-

ful persecution ensued, of which the venerable Schall
was one of the earliest victims. He was charged
with having exhibited a crucifix to Chunchi upon his
deathbed, that sovereign having then sent for him
and listened with apparent humility to the consola-
tions which he offered. The aged man with three of
his companions were loaded with irons, and during
nine months led about from one tribunal to another,
and finally condemned to be strangled and cut to
pieces. In the midst of these trials, father Verbiest,
regardless of his own troubles, exerted all his eloquence in behalf of one whom he respected as his
master. He pleaded the virtues of Schall, and the
services which he had rendered to the court for so
long a period. All his arguments, however, were
futile, till a curious concurrence of accidents, viz.,
the appearance of a comet, an earthquake, and the
breaking out of a fire which consumed a great portion of the imperial palace, produced the impression
that these were marks of the displeasure of Providence, and the prisoners were set at liberty. The
venerable Schall, however, sunk under his trials,
being struck with paralysis, and died at the advanced
age of seventy-eight.

On Kang-hi attaining his majority in 1671, he
appointed Verbiest as the successor of Schall in the
department of astronomy, and allowed the missionaries to return to their stations. It is not improba-
ble, that the important service rendered by him in
correcting the Chinese calendar, was the leading
cause in this restoration to favour. An intercalary

month had been erroneously inserted by the ignorance of the Chinese astronomers, which his intelligent observation showed him the necessity of striking
out, so that to the great surprise of the people the
year was abridged by the length of one month. The
emperor himself was anxious to take lessons of him in
mathematics, and at his request Verbiest made himself
master of the Tartar language, in order to dispense
with an interpreter in communicating his instruction.
Besides the services of a literary and scientific nature
which this talented missionary was able to offer to
the emperor, there was one of a more practical kind
in which he assisted him most effectually. In 1681
he was desired by the emperor to superintend the
casting of artillery.   In this novel occupation he was
again equally successful, and he had the satisfaction
of offering the emperor a park of three hundred and
twenty pieces of his own manufacture. It may well
be judged with what gratitude these various bene-
ficial services would be received by an emperor such
as Kang-hi, whose high qualities have rendered him
more celebrated than almost any other Asiatic sovereign ; nor can we doubt the correctness of the
statements which father Verbiest has here given us
respecting the gracious bearing of the sovereign
towards himself and brother missionaries.

The maintenance of the military character of the Tartars, by which their final establishment on the throne
of China was secured, was in a great measure due to
the emperor's frequent hunting excursions beyond the
Great Wall, thereby exposing them to fatigues and

dangers, in many respects analogous to the trials of actual warfare. The correctness of a remark upon this subject by Sir John Davis, has been so strikingly shown by recent events as to appear prophetic. He says, " It is worthy of remark, that, of the score of dynasties which have followed each other, all established themselves on the vices, luxury, or indolence of their immediate forerunners. The present Manchou race has already shown no unequivocal symptoms of degeneracy. The two greatest princes by whom it has been distinguished, Kang-hi and Kien-loong, sedulously maintained the ancient habits of their Tartar subjects by frequent hunting excursions beyond the wall, in which they individually bore no small share of the fatigue and danger. The late emperor, Keaking, and the present one, have, on the other hand, been remarkable for their comparative indolence ; and the reigns of both have exhibited a mere succession of revolts and troubles. The following is part of an edict issued by the reigning monarch in 1824 :—' With reference to the autumnal hunt of the present year, I ought to follow the established custom of my predecessors ; but, at the same time, it is necessary to be guided by the circumstances of the times, and to act in conformity to them. The expedition to Je-ho (Zhehol) is also ordered to be put off for this year. It is an involuntary source of vexation to me : I should not think of adopting this measure from a love of ease and indulgence.' Since that date, however, the same course has been repeated under various pretexts. The Manchou rule has already lasted much longer than the Mongol, and, from all present appearances, a bold Chinese adventurer might perhaps succeed in overthrowing it." In two of these hunting excursions Verbiest was desired to accompany the train of the emperor, and, indeed, was frequently closely attendant upon his person. His two letters, in which these journeys are respectively described, were regarded with great in terest on their arrival in Europe. The originals, in all probability, were written in Latin; for although Verbiest was a Fleming, and many of the Jesuit narratives were written in other languages than Latin, yet Dutch, we may conclude, would be less acceptable to those to whom the letters were sent than Latin, with which the writer was so perfectly conversant. They were translated into French, and published at Paris in 1685, 16mo., and in the preface to this little work, the anonymous editor asserts that they are translated word for word from the originals. A translation from this French version was published in the *Philosophical Transactions* of the Royal Society, in the number for March and April, 1686. This French version also was reprinted by Père d'Orleans in the work now translated.

While we can thus only speak with uncertainty as to the language of the original documents, it is worthy of remark that the Dutch version, inserted by the celebrated burgomaster Nicholas Witsen (himself a long time resident in Tartary), in his "Noord en Oost Tartarye", shows considerable variations in many parts, from the language as given in the French. It therefore remains a question whether the Dutch presented to us by Witsen is the language of the original letters, or whether Witsen himself had newly translated the letters and made his own alterations. In either case it has been deemed desirable to supply a translation from the Dutch, and the editor has therefore given it in the form of appendix.

The first appearance of Witsen's work was at Amsterdam in 1692, folio. The French version was also inserted in the fourth volume of the " Recueil des Voyages au Nord", Amst. 1732, 16mo., and also in the fourth volume of Du Halde's " Description de la Chine et de la Tartarie Chinoise", Paris, 1735-6, 4to. Father Verbiest continued to enjoy the imperial favour till his death, on the 7th of February, 1688, and so great was the grief at his loss, and the respect paid to him, that his funeral was not only attended by a large concourse of his fellow missionaries, but by mandarins especially appointed by the emperor to do honour to the occasion.

His place as Superintendent of the Board of Mathematics was supplied by father Pereira, a Jesuit who, like himself, stood high in the emperor's regard on account of his scientific attainments. One branch of science in especial, the knowledge of instrumental music and skill in constructing musical instruments, which he seemed to possess in a high degree, had a great charm for the emperor, and in order that he might study this science under such excellent tuition he took the learned father with him, as stated at page 96, on one of the frequent hunting excursions of which we have already been speaking. A most interesting description of this journey in a letter from his own hand, the Dutch translation of which is also given by Witsen in his great work on North and East Tartary, is added to this volume as an additional appendix, its translation and publication in this place having been considered for every reason especially desirable.

The Père d'Orleans, himself a Jesuit, to whom France is indebted for various well-written works,—all of which, strangely enough, excepting his sermons, are on subjects connected with revolution,—has in the present volume given us a succinct and interesting compilation, the materials of which he makes us acquainted with in the "Avertissement" to the volume. The work is now become extremely scarce. At the close of the "Avertissement", the author makes some judicious remarks respecting the mode of representing Chinese names in European languages. In conformity with the sense of those remarks, we have appended a list of the names which occur in the volume, with the mode of representing them in English as given us by Morrison.

Dynasty Ta-Ming, or Tae-Ming, or Ming.

Book the First.

25.	Venchui	Wăn-Shwuy.
26.	Chamienchon	Sha-mëen-chung ?
30.	Icoan	E-Kwang ?
31.	Quesin	Kwei-sing ?
33.	Lam	Lang.
35.	Mafa, Manchoo Tartar (Ancestor)	Same in English. Also p. 122.
44.	Camhi	Kang-he.

Book the Second.

51.	Sukama	Soo-këa-ma ?
46.	Yam-quam-Sien	Yang-kwang-Sëen, or Yang-kang-Sëen.
54.	Yonnan	Yunnan.
57.	Kenvan	Ken-wang ?
59.	Kiamsi	Këang-se.
59.	Kienchamp	Këen-chang.
59.	Sumvan	Sung-wang ?
51.	Chin	Chin or Ching ?
52.	Gantacum	Gan-ta-kung.
71.	Ula	Oola.
71.	Songoro	Songgoro.
71.	Sumpoa	Sung-hwa.
75.	Xim-yam	Shing-yang.
73.	Kam-hay	Kang-hae.
74.	Pequeli	Pĭh-che-le.
76.	Champe	Chang-pĭh, or Chang-pĭh-sham—(The long White Mountain).

HISTOIRE

DES

DEUX CONQUERANS

TARTARES

QUI ONT SUBJUGUÉ

LA CHINE,

Par le R. P. PIERRE JOSEPH D'ORLEANS,
de la Compagnie de Jesus.

A PARIS,

CHEZ CLAUDE BARBIN, AU PALAIS SUR LE SECOND PERRON DE LA SAINTE CHAPELLE.

M.DC.LXXXVIII.

AVEC PRIVILEGE DU ROY.

DEDICATION

TO

MY LORD THE CHANCELLOR.

My Lord,

Among the rarities of China, there are none which better deserve to be presented to persons of your rank and taste, than those which I here offer to you. China has nothing to surpass the history of the two kings who conquered it; and the rest of the world would have had nothing to equal it, if Louis the Great had not reigned in France.

The conquest of so many provinces is the least important point in their history which claims our admiration. The former commenced that course of conquest at eight years of age, the second completed it at fourteen : it is a miracle of their good fortune rather than an effect of their virtue. But that which cannot be sufficiently admired, and which I am sure, my lord, will interest you much, is the wisdom of these monarchs in governing this vast empire, and the infinite multitude of people which Heaven has subjected to their administration.

There cannot be any one better fitted than yourself to appreciate their wisdom, and therefore I have thought that I could not present the portrait of these two heroes to the eyes of any person more capable than yourself of rightly estimating their virtues. That clear intelligence which has so long enlightened your career in so many different occupations, without your having hitherto taken any of those dangerous steps which the most clear-sighted cannot always avoid, will cause you to follow with pleasure, in the conduct of these princes, the traces of a policy which has been skilful without cunning, and efficacious without violence. The

inflexible equity which you profess, and which has induced
the most just of kings to place you at the head of all the
tribunals of justice in his kingdom, must awaken your esteem
for those conquerors, who during their conquests held the
balance while they wielded the sword, and seemed only to
gain subjects in order that they might dispense happiness to
a greater number of people. Great without pride, strict
without rigour, exact observers of the laws, but without that
cruel harshness which excites hatred while it establishes
authority, you will admire in them that pliancy of genius
which has been able at the same time to civilize the Tartar
warriors, and to socialize the emperors of China.

Your zeal for religion, my lord, will cause you to regret
that the one should have died an idolator, and that the other
should not yet be a Christian : but if in this you find some
grounds for regret, you will also find abundant reason to
praise them for the liberty which they have allowed to their
people to profess Christianity, and for the powerful protection
with which they have always honoured those who preached it.
God, who holds in His hand the hearts of kings, has His own
time for touching them : the obligations under which we lie
to the prince who now reigns in China, make us pray that
that time may be hastened, as those which we owe to you,
my lord, make us pray God for the continuance of the blessings which He pours upon you ; viz., the preservation of the
health so precious to all the state, the prosperity of the illustrious family so worthy to have you for its chief, the confidence of the prince, the love of the people, the approbation
of all good men. If my *work* does not merit your approbation, concede it at least to the sincere zeal, and to the very
profound respect with which I am,

My Lord,

Your very humble and obedient servant,

Pierre Joseph d'Orléans,

Of the Order of Jesus.

PREFACE.

In the letters which we receive from different parts of the
world, where the labourers of the gospel have been sent to
proclaim the faith to the Gentiles, or to bring again into
obedience to the vicar of Jesus Christ those whom schism
has withdrawn, two kinds of subjects are treated of. The
principal are those which relate immediately to religion ; the
progress it has made, the persecutions it suffers, and the
means of extending or of preserving it. This has hitherto
been the subject of the accounts which have been given, in
order to show to those who help with their prayers or with
their charity the works of apostolic men, what blessing God
has bestowed upon them.

This will hereafter be of service to an illustrious ecclesiastic, to establish the faith of the Christians and Catholics
of France, by the history of the progress which that faith is
making among the idolators of the Indies or the schismatics
of the Levant. The king, who adds to the glory of his heroic
actions the merit of so many works of goodness, has issued
an express injunction, that the public should every year be
made acquainted with all that is learned of this nature calculated to animate the zeal and the charity of good souls,
and to induce them to concur with him in reuniting in one
flock all the wandering sheep. The ecclesiastic of whom I
speak has expressed his willingness to undertake this duty,
which is to him an agreeable occupation, and which gives
him the means of contributing something to a work, which
he regards as the greatest possible benefit that can be done
to religion. The inclination which he has always shown for
this kind of· thing, has caused him to make connections and
establish an epistolary correspondence with almost all the

missionaries that have left France during the last ten years. Thus he works from his own documents, which, coming from the same sources as ours, only differ from them in the terms employed. Whatever study I may have given to these matters, I have not been able to compete with a man of so great merit as he of whom I speak, nor thought it safe for my reputation to write on the same subjects as a person of such accomplishments as he possesses.

It is then in order to leave this field free to him, that I confine myself to the other class of subjects which are dealt with in these letters from distant countries. I have extracted from them all that could give a more perfect knowledge of the situation and nature of those countries, as well as the history and manners of the nations who inhabit them. What I have given in these two volumes, is only a trial to prove whether this kind of work will be successful, so that I may judge by the reception given to them whether I am to continue or cease to work at them.

I commence by the history of the two conquerors who have in our own days subjugated China,—the late emperor, and he who at present reigns with so much honour. In that of the first, I follow in many things the fathers Martini and de Rougemont; but more especially the letters of father Adam Schall, who has been at the court of this prince, and shared his confidence and even taken part in his education, and whose memoirs for this reason appeared to me not only to be more depended upon than the others, but more in accordance with my design, which is less to make a history of the reign of these monarchs, than a history of their personal conduct. I have taken nothing from Palafox. A man who wrote the " History of China" in Mexico on information sent to him from the Philippines, could not be a good guide to follow, above all when there are a sufficient number of eye-witnesses of these things, and who have only written that which they have seen.

As regards the present emperor, I have taken all that I have said from letters which have come to us every year from China, and as much as I could from those of father Ferdinand Verbiest, whom this prince honoured with his kindness, and with whom he lived somewhat on the same terms as his predecessor had done with father Adam. The father Adrian Greslon, a Frenchman, has taken more pains than any one else in collecting whatever regards the history of the country, and I owe to one of his relations all that I relate of the last league of the Chinese mandarins against the Tartar domination.

Those who shall write the history of China, or who may continue that of father Martini, which learned men expect of the Jesuits of Pekin as soon as they shall have leisure to do it, will doubtless in it find matter worthy of the public curiosity, such as great wars, great revolutions, a tolerably well sustained system of policy, heroic virtue in some, philosophy in most : but among so many things that are calculated to please and instruct the reader, there are two rocks which they will have to avoid.

The first is the rendering their history obscure by loading it with a great number of actors, whose proper names are as difficult to distinguish, as their qualities are unknown to those who have not studied them for a long time. It is as much as one can do to unravel these things in the history of Greece or of Rome, and even yet there are but few people who give themselves the trouble. So that all that historians gain by this exactness in wishing to give the names and employments of all those of whom they have occasion to speak, is to leave the reader ignorant of the persons whom he ought to know, while he is made acquainted with those of whom it would signify little if he were ignorant. If it happens thus in history which every one wishes to know, how much more likely it is to happen in those which excite less curiosity, and of which even the learned may continue ignorant without disgrace.

The second rock on which those who write the history of China may split, is the giving a bad pronunciation to the reader, by following out the Chinese orthography in every language. For as the Chinese pronounce certain letters differently to us, it will consequently happen that we shall have no Chinese name as it ought to be pronounced.

To remedy these inconveniences, I have observed two things in this work. Firstly, I have suppressed a great number of names of little use to the understanding of my history, and which would very much have diminished its chance of pleasing. In the second place, I have reduced to our orthography those which I have been obliged to put, writing them rather as we ought to pronounce them, than as they ought to be written according to the Chinese orthography. Thus I have written *Chunchi*, and not *Xunchi;* because the Chinese pronounce this *x* as we pronounce *ch*.

I have made a mistake in writing Taisu, a famous person in the Chinese history, which they pronounce as if it had a *z*, while it ought to be pronounced as if it had two *ss*, because in following the Chinese orthography most exactly, Tai-çu should be written with a *c* and a cedilla. To remedy this it should have been written Taissu, or Tai-su.

The name of the present emperor embarrasses me. He is called Camhi, and the last syllable of his name appeared to me, when I heard it pronounced by a Chinese who was a long time resident in this house, to have the same sound as the Spanish consonant *j* in the words Juan, Hijo, and the like ; so that to write it in French as nearly as possible to represent the Chinese pronunciation, the best mode would be to spell it Canqui, breathing a little on the last syllable. But I have been afraid of disguising the word too much, and have come to the conclusion that it was better it should run the risk of being badly pronounced than to be altogether misunderstood.

THE HISTORY

OF THE

TARTAR CONQUERORS WHO SUBDUED

CHINA.

THERE is something so singular in the history of the two
celebrated conquerors who subdued China, that we can
scarcely give to the public anything more curious and agreeable than the information we have acquired concerning the
great actions of these monarchs. Their genius, their courage, and their general conduct, were alike remarkable ; and
it will be seen by what we are about to relate, that the
politeness of these Tartar kings would be held in as high
estimation in France as in China.

In order to explain more clearly all the circumstances
which have any connexion with them, I shall begin their
history by giving some account of their ancestors, who set
on foot those extensive conquests which our heroes brought
to such a successful termination, and the fruits of which, as
we learn, the present sovereign peaceably enjoys.

In that vast territory which bears the name of Tartary, is Two kinds of Tartars,
situated, on the north of China, an extensive country divided the ancient enemies of
into two provinces, which, in allusion to the position they China.
occupy in reference to one another, have been named Eastern and Western Tartary. The former is also known by
the name of the kingdom of Niuché, the latter by that of
the kingdom of Tanyu. A deep-seated rivalry has always

1

existed between these nations and the Chinese, and the famous
Wall, which was built two thousand years ago, was found
insufficient to prevent the recurrence of sanguinary wars.
Fortune has repeatedly favoured the Chinese, and yet it has

The Tartars
have twice
subdued
China.
now happened for the second time that they have been compelled to bow beneath the Tartar yoke. These two events are
so closely connected, and a knowledge of the former is so
necessary to the right comprehension of the latter, that I
should be depriving the reader of one of the greatest charms
of this history were I to omit the recital of it.

China was
first con-
quered by
the Tartars
in 1100.
At the beginning of the twelfth century, under the reign
of an emperor of China named Hoïsson, the inhabitants
of the province of Leauton, having adopted the warlike
habits of their neighbours the Eastern Tartars, began to
harass the other parts of the empire by frequent maraud-
ing incursions. The emperor wished to suppress these dis-
orders, but he found the authors of them intractable; they
defeated the troops that he sent against them, and they pushed
on their conquests so far, that the emperor was forced to apply
for assistance to those very neighbours who had taught them
the art of war in order to compel them to live in peace.
The aid thus solicited was promptly afforded, for the Tartars
only require sufficient time for their preparations to allow
them to put on their armour. They marched against the
rebels, and hemming them in between their own army and
that of the Chinese, which advanced from the opposite
quarter, they very speedily reduced them to submission.

Pekin rang with the shouts of victory, but the inhabitants
were extremely surprised to learn that the Tartars, instead
of accepting the usual expressions of gratitude with the
accompanying presents, demanded a portion of the empire,
which they boasted to have sustained when on the brink
of ruin. There was but one course left to pursue with respect to those who held such language. An appeal to arms
was inevitable; but the gilt weapons of the Chinese were

far inferior in temper to the Tartar cutlasses; the former were defeated in more than one pitched battle, and were obliged to yield to force what they had refused to surrender on agreement.

The Tartars made themselves masters of Pekin and of the adjoining provinces. The emperor was betrayed into the hands of his enemies, who sent him to one of the deserts of Tartary, where he died. His successor was also taken during a siege, and underwent a similar fate, in consequence of which the third was obliged to retreat to the southern provinces, and there to hold his court.

The whole of Northern China continued for one hundred and fifty years under the dominion of these new rulers, during which time every effort made by the Chinese to shake off the yoke proved unsuccessful. In their despair the children, forgetting the errors of their fathers, like them called in the aid of a powerful enemy to drive out a weaker one. For a long time the Western Tartars had left the Chinese unmolested: and the signal successes which an emperor of China named Vuti had obtained over them, had left them so weak, that they seemed to have lost all desire of recrossing the boundary of the Great Wall. The Chinese themselves, however, revived this inclination, at a time when the idea of it was least present to their thoughts, by imploring their aid, and by entering into an alliance with them for the purpose of driving out the Eastern Tartars. These last were made acquainted with this negotiation soon enough to have been able to prevent its completion, if the Chinese had chosen to listen to the terms of an agreement which was proposed; but the emperor and his ministers having declined to entertain the proposals, there remained no alternative left but a resort to arms. The defenders maintained an obstinate resistance, and there were instances in which towns held out for such a length of time, that the besieged were reduced to the extremity of eating one another; so that, to speak correctly, they were

rather exterminated than expelled. The last of their kings,
Negayti, died by his own hand. The remainder escaped
with difficulty, and returned to their former homes. It is
said, that when their sovereign sent to the emperor of China
to ask for conditions of peace, he added these words: "Those
whom you summon to your assistance will deprive me of my
kingdom, but after they have deprived me of my own, they
will deprive you of yours." The event proved that his pre-
diction was but too true, the Western Tartars only drove out
the others in order to fill their place, and as with equal ambition they possessed far more power, not satisfied with their
share of the empire, they resolved to get possession of that
portion which the Chinese still retained. They accordingly
declared war, and prosecuted it with such vigour under the
conduct of their king, Chisu, and of another celebrated captain called Peyen, that in twenty years they had driven back
the Chinese emperors to the very limits of the empire.

The last of these monarchs, named Tipin, a boy of eight or
ten years old, was compelled to retire to the sea shore, where
his armed fleet, which formed his last resource, having been
defeated by that of the Tartars in 1281, his general seized
the child in his arms and plunged with him into the sea.

Chisu remaining thus master of the empire, became the
founder of that royal house which the Chinese call the
dynasty of Yven, which though originally of alien and
Tartar extraction, nevertheless became so popular, that to
this day the people call it the holy, and fondly cherish it in
their memory.

The Chinese
drive out the
Tartars.
However mild a form of government may be, there are
always persons who, either from a spirit of rebellion, or
from natural restlessness, grow impatient under it. Hardly
sixty years had elapsed since the dynasty of Yven had ascended the throne of China, when a conspiracy was formed
to expel it. The chief mover in the enterprise was a person
of good fortune named Taisu. He had been servant to a

bonze, and had left that employment to place himself at the head of a band of reckless men, who wandered about the country for plunder. The successes he achieved in this petty warfare, inspired him with the idea that he was capable of undertaking one on a larger scale. Unfortunately for the Tartars, Chunti, who was now upon the throne, though a well-disposed prince, had not, in addition to other good qualities, inherited the talents or abilities of his ancestors. He was superstitious, addicted to pleasure, and negligent of public affairs, which he abandoned to the management of a minister as incapable as himself. Taisu, who was gifted with remarkable talents, together with courage and resolution, having become aware of this condition of the Tartar sovereign's affairs in China, took his measures to profit by it, and the scheme he conceived was no less than that of dethroning the sovereign and substituting himself as emperor.

Having formed this project he sounded the dispositions of his companions, who declared themselves ready to follow him; he began operations by attacking the towns in the southern provinces, which, being furthest from the seat of Government, were also, in consequence, more remote from succour. He was so successful in his first attacks, that, in a very short time, he found himself in a condition to carry all before him; and, what was most to his advantage, his army gained fresh reinforcements from every place he took, the people all vying with one another for the honour of enrolling themselves under the banner of public liberty. Thus he saw himself all at once master of a considerable number of places, and general of a large army.

The sensation made by these successes could not fail to rouse Chunti from slumber; but it was too late. Taisu, meeting with no further obstacle, marched so rapidly towards the capital, that he did not even give his enemy territory enough to draw resources from for retrieving a single defeat in a pitched battle. Thus the first battle, being won by

Taisu, decided the fate of both combatants. Chunti fled;
and finding only safety in the territory of his ancestors,
retired thither, and died there two years afterwards. Taisu
found himself master of the empire; in the possession of
which he remained undisturbed, being judged worthy of
it, no less in virtue of conquest than of his high qualities.
He took the name of Humvu, which signifies, Great Warrior; and was the head of the royal family of Taimin which
has existed nearly three hundred years, and has given six-
teen emperors to China.

During the reigns of the first twelve of these princes,
though the Tartars had, after their habit, from time to time,
made war against the Chinese, and had even been often successful; yet the Chinese had always driven them back beyond
the Great Wall, which was constantly guarded, even in time
of peace, by a million of troops. It is said that the emperor, Vanlié, had not scrupled to make use of money
as well as arms; and that he had not considered it deroga-
tory to the dignity of the Chinese empire to purchase tranquillity for his dominions and the repose of his subjects by
the payment of a kind of pension to the Tartars of Tanyu.

The Tartars re-enter China in the reign of the emperor Vanlié.   In spite of these precautions for securing peace, it was
during the reign of this prince that the sanguinary war was
begun, which has since produced so many revolutions. Till
then, he had been one of the most fortunate, as well as one
of the greatest, monarchs that had ever occupied the throne
of China. Beloved by his subjects, feared by his enemies,
respected by all the eastern sovereigns—many of whom paid
tribute to him—his prosperity was unequalled. One cannot

The Christian religion preached in China.   doubt that these blessings are attributable, in a great measure,
to the favourable reception he gave to the ministers of the
Gospel; for it was in the beginning of his reign that the
celebrated jesuit, Matthew Ricci, first introduced the Christian religion into this great empire.

We may safely say, that the victories he gained for the

cause of Christianity, were made at a higher cost than those which the Tartars achieved in the service of their monarch. For, at every step, he had to encounter obstacles which he would have found insurmountable but for the heroic courage which in him was combined with the patience of an apostle. His perseverance prevailed over all, and he was finally enabled to insinuate himself into the good graces of the emperor. He employed his credit at court, with success, to effect the establishment of Christianity in the empire; he obtained the importation of a considerable number of missionaries of his order; he founded numerous churches; and he had, upon his deathbed, the consolation of seeing many of the Mandarins converted to Christianity. He died in 1610, leaving religion already flourishing in China.

Together with religion, the secular affairs of the empire also prospered; till Vanlié, at the suggestion of some of his officers, dried up its source, and arrested the progress of the faith by banishing the missionaries. He soon after had the mortification of seeing the lustre of his reign tarnished by the kindling of those wars which resulted in placing strangers upon his throne, and reducing his people to servitude. *Vanlié banishes the ministers of the gospel, and is punished by a revolution.*

This revolution, which broke out in the year 1616, owed its origin to the vexatious oppressions which the Tartars of Niuché suffered from the governors of those Chinese towns which are situated on their frontier. It was only a few years before that these Tartars had erected a kingdom, composed of six or seven petty states, whose several rulers, after incessantly quarrelling among themselves, had finally determined to submit quietly to the one who proved the strongest. The Chinese governors who, in accordance with the ancient customs of the empire, exercised absolute authority, and who, moreover, deemed it consistent with their policy to repress this growing power, had spared no effort to thwart their commerce and their alliances; and having even, by some stratagem, possessed themselves of the person of their king, they had put him to a cruel death. *Commencement of the revolution.*

Fortunately for his dominions, this prince had a son old enough to succeed him, who, in order to show himself worthy of the throne, began his reign by undertaking to revenge the death of his father. Accordingly he raised an army, and making a sudden inroad into the province of Leauton, took possession of Cayven, the principal town, and spread terror throughout the country. He might have pursued these advantages, had not a latent feeling of respect for the Chinese empire induced him to seek a gentler means of obtaining satisfaction for the murder of his father, by complaining to the emperor himself, a just prince, and who, he well knew, was no party to the excesses which were committed by the governors. Having adopted this resolution, he despatched a messenger to Pekin, bearing a letter couched in respectful terms; in which, after laying before the emperor the wrongs he had endured from his ministers, he justified the course of action he had adopted, and excused the invasion of the emperor's dominions on the plea that he had been inflamed by a just impulse of grief. He farther proceeded to assure the emperor he was prepared to restore the places he had taken, and to lead back his troops beyond the wall, provided he could obtain a favourable hearing, and that the emperor would act up to his professions of justice, by himself punishing the violence committed by his subjects. This letter never reached Vanlié, as the Tartar chief had fondly hoped. For whether it was that this prince, already advanced in age, had begun to retire from public affairs, or that he considered this transaction as an event beneath his notice, certain it is that he made over the case to his ministers; who, far from considering themselves under the necessity of appeasing the insulted prince, were highly displeased that he should have presumed to complain of them to their master.

The Tartar, irritated at the contempt shown him by the emperor, and at the insolent treatment of his ministers,

vowed the destruction of the Chinese empire, and, urged by
the dictates of a barbarous piety, he took an oath to sacrifice,
to the manes of his father, the blood of 200,000 Chinese.
In this frame of mind he sprang on his horse, marched at
once upon the capital of the province of Leauton, besieged
and reduced it; and taking advantage of the consternation
which the report of his victories had spread among the
people, penetrated into the province of Pekin, and advanced
to within seven leagues of the seat of the empire, sparing
every town that surrendered, and mercilessly putting to fire
and sword those that dared to offer resistance. This done,
he might have ventured to lay siege to Pekin; but this
sagacious warrior, unwilling to trust too much to chance for
success, considered that he had done enough for the present;
and, fearing lest he should be hemmed in by the numerous
troops which the Chinese were assembling from all parts, he
retreated into the Leauton laden with the spoils of two rich
provinces, and as if certain that his successes would equal
his ambition, he took the title of emperor of China, with the
Chinese surname of Thienmin.

The victory which he obtained shortly afterwards, confirmed him in his hopes. For the Chinese having assembled
an army of 600,000 men, he defeated them in a pitched
battle, and leaving 50,000 of them dead upon the field, he
pursued the remainder as far as Pekin itself. Had he attacked it, he would no doubt have succeeded in effecting an
entrance; for the panic was so great that the emperor himself would have quitted it to fly into the southern provinces,
had not his council represented to him that such a proceeding would be a disgrace to himself and a heavy discourage-
ment to his subjects, whereas it could not fail to embolden
his enemies. It was not the will of heaven that the emperor
should terminate his reign and his life in such a state of de-
gradation. He did not long survive the decline of his power,
having, indeed, deserved his fate by the culpable weakness

Thienmin the first Tartar king who enters China.

2

with which, at the instigation of his ministers, he had allowed the preachers of the gospel to be driven from his dominions. It would at the same time appear, that he was spared from witnessing the final downfall of the empire, on account of his having always favoured the cause of Christianity, and of his having been the first Chinese emperor who had permitted that faith to be preached.

Death of Vanlié.

Vanlié expired in the year 1620, after a reign of forty-seven years. He was succeeded by his son Taichau, who followed him to the grave almost as soon as to the throne. He reigned only four months, leaving the crown to one of his children, named Thienhi, who possessed the abilities requisite to have repaired the losses of the state, had his reign been longer. He infused into his subjects such a spirit of universal ardour for the defence of their common country, that not only was China moved with a universal enthusiasm, but the surrounding nations caught the infection. The king of Corea supplied him with some good troops, and a queen, who reigned in the mountains of Suchuen, appeared leading her reinforcements in person, the king her son being as yet too young to bear arms. This princess afforded proofs that virtues of the highest order are confined to no sex or country, for she performed feats in this war of which the greatest captains might be proud, and which in ancient times would have ranked her amongst the most renowned of Amazons.

The ministers of the gospel are recalled.

Two Christian mandarins considered this occasion to be favourable for obtaining the recall of the preachers of the gospel, and suggested to the emperor to apply to the Portuguese of Macao to send him persons more expert than the Chinese in the management of artillery, of which the latter were very ignorant. Their scheme was entirely successful; the preachers were recalled, and the emperor annulled the decree of banishment pronounced against them by his grandfather, and even allowed them to add several to their num-

ber. But he was not compelled to wait for the assistance of
the Portuguese to commence hostilities. For, happily, the
Tartar king being occupied in his own dominions, Thienki
took such immediate advantage of this circumstance, and of
the good spirit that prevailed amongst the Chinese, whom
the cruelty of the Tartars had considerably alienated, that
he regained possession of a great part of the territory which
had been wrested from him.

These successes were not lasting: ere long, the Tartar
prince had concluded the business which detained him in
his own country, and recrossing the Wall at the head of a
powerful army, he recovered in a short time all the places
which the Chinese had taken.

Notwithstanding the characteristic effeminacy of the Instance of constancy in a Chinese.
Chinese, we might cite many instances occurring in the
course of this war, of that constancy which we admire in the
ancient Romans. The following is one of the most remarkable. A Chinese grandee, who had been taken prisoner
during a siege, was led before the Tartar king, and required
to acknowledge this prince as his sovereign. The prisoner
was doubtless well aware that a refusal would be followed
by no less than death, and that the only mercy he could
expect was that his enemies should spare his constancy the
trial of lingering torture. The Tartars, who had met with
much pusillanimity amongst the Chinese and very little
loyalty to their sovereign, were far from expecting any resistance in the present instance. But they were all taken
by surprise when the mandarin, with a noble bearing which
would have done honour to a Roman consul, replied to their
demand that he was incapable of rendering to a stranger the
honour which was due to his own sovereign alone, and that
if the fortune of war had unhappily placed his life at the
mercy of the Tartar, it had nevertheless left his heart and
principles free. True virtue always inspires respect, the
Tartars were struck with admiration in this instance, and

feeling ashamed of detaining him longer in prison, they restored the courageous mandarin to liberty and sent him back
to his emperor. His well-tried fidelity deserved the highest
praise and reward; but a custom prevailed in China at that
time that every general who had been unfortunate should be
treated as culpable, a severity which had become necessary
on account of the frequent treachery practised by the mandarins. Consequently, our hero considered that he owed it
to his country to resign himself to this law, and died by his
own act to avoid a less honourable fate at the hands of others.

Fidelity of a
Christian
Mandarin. This severe discipline afforded an opportunity to a Christian chieftain named Sun, of honouring his religion by a
rare instance of fidelity to his king and his country. He
commanded an army in Leauton, at this time the theatre of
war, and which he governed as viceroy. He had gained
some important victories, and nothing was wanting to make
him the most fortunate captain of his time, but to be better
assisted by the court, which did not even allow him money
to pay his troops.

The severity of his virtue had been the cause of this treatment, for he would never condescend, like others, to purchase the favour of the ministers by unworthy means, or to
corrupt their integrity by presents. Consequently, it was
in vain that he represented to them the state to which his
army was reduced for want of pay: his demands remained
unanswered. Beloved as he was by his souldiers, he averted
for some time by his authority alone the evil effects of their
murmurs; but at last their patience was exhausted—a mutiny
broke out, they took the general by surprise, made themselves masters of a town and pillaged it. Their fury having
subsided, they saw that their general's fate was sealed, and
that the only means of saving him was to raise the standard
of rebellion and entirely shake off the yoke. They spared no
efforts to incite him to this course of action, promising to
follow him implicitly, and declaring that they would not res

till they had placed him on the throne of China. The general saw that his own destruction and that of his soldiers was inevitable, and he knew well that the only chance he had of saving his head was to follow the line of conduct which was recommended to him. Far, however, from complying with their suggestions, he forcibly represented to them the enormity of the crime in which they had sought to involve him, and not only succeeded in regaining all his influence over their minds, but even had the courage to punish the authors of the revolt.

This noble conduct, which excited the admiration of all classes in the empire, met with nothing but censure from the court, where the news of these events had no sooner been received than a summons was despatched to Sun, requiring him to answer for his conduct before the emperor, while a successor was despatched to supersede him.

The army was filled with consternation at this news, and every argument was employed to induce the general to resist the order. "Do not leave us," they entreated, "we will undertake to defend you from your calumniators. It is our cause, leave it to us." While his soldiers were thus pressing him, the Tartar prince, who had been informed of what was passing, sent to offer him a refuge in his dominions, assuring him of protection if he would consent to join his party. Amidst all these sore temptations, the general listened only to the voice of his conscience, and exhorting his troops to follow the example of his fidelity, he tore himself from their arms to place himself voluntarily in the hands of his enemies, who, unmoved by an instance of such wonderful heroism, mercilessly condemned to death one who was worthy to live.

Many similar examples occurred during this war in which the Christian religion was honoured, either by her open professors, or by those who, having associated with them, had adopted their precepts.

A celebrated chief called Mauvenlon was amongst the

latter. He was a native of the province of Canton, where
he had had dealings with the Portuguese. From them he
had learnt the art of war, and, at the same time, those true
principles of loyalty to one's king and one's country, which
are ever inculcated by true religion. Moreover, no one
more firmly resisted the solicitations of the Tartars, who
carried their intrigues so far as to promise him a division of
the empire if he would assist them to conquer it. The efforts
that he made to arrest their progress, proved that he was
invulnerable to this temptation. He was not invariably
successful, but in every reverse he had so many resources to
fall back upon, that if he did not always come off victorious,
his enemies could never boast of having vanquished him. It
was thus that he maintained in the emperor's interest the
king and kingdom of Corea, where he repeatedly defeated
the Tartars, and where they obtained over him but a few
doubtful successes. He perished through the perfidy of a
certain Yven, who poisoned him in order to rid himself of an
obstacle to his treasonable designs against his sovereign, who
had confided to him the government of the province of
Leauton. The secret communications which this traitor
carried on with the Tartars narrowly failed to overthrow the
empire, for he made no attempt to interfere with their proceedings : they entered Pequeli, laid siege to Pekin, and
would have taken the town, were it not that the treason of
Yven having been discovered, his well-merited death so
terrified them, that they hastened to fall back upon their
The Tartars earlier conquests. From that time all their efforts to extend
repulsed. them were vigorously repulsed, both during the reign of
Thienmin their first leader, and of Thienson who succeeded
him.

They had subsided into a state of quiescence, especially
after an individual named Usanquey had been appointed to
command the army which the emperor maintained on the
frontier to oppose their inroads, when the divisions amongst
the Chinese opened to them anew the doors of the empire.

In the year 1636, during the reigns of Zonchin in China, Robbers
trouble
the successor of Thienki, and of Zunké in Tartary, successor China with
a revolt.
to Thienson, a band of robbers collected in the mountains
of Suchüen, and began to lay waste that province. The
Amazon of whom we have already spoken defeated them,
but she did not succeed in exterminating them. In consequence of the defection of one of the mandarins, who was
smarting under some injustice, their numbers were swelled
by the addition of all his partisans, while the avarice of the
emperor, who during a severe famine refused to lighten in
the smallest degree the burden of the taxes, multiplied the
robbers to that extent, that separating under two independent leaders, they made themselves masters of the open country and shortly after of the large towns.

The most considerable of these chieftains, named Licon, Licon, chief
of the rebels,
after having made trial of his arms in several combats, in makes war
against the
which he always came off victorious, had at length the auda- emperor.
city to besiege the emperor in his own capital. Unfortunately for this prince his court was torn by factions. He
had succeeded in ridding himself of a eunuch called Guey,
having grown jealous of his power; for his predecessor had
loaded him with favours so far as to raise him to an office in
the government. This eunuch had a faction of his own
hostile to the emperor, and hoping that the approach of the
rebels would afford him an opportunity of revenging himself, he favoured the projects of Licon and facilitated his
entry into the town and the palace.

The unfortunate Zonchin perished, not by the weapons of Death of
Zonchin,
his revolted subjects, but by his own hand, for he hanged emperor of
China.
himself to a tree by his shoe-ties. His empress and those
faithful attendants who remained at his side, voluntarily submitted to the same fate.

He left three sons and one daughter. Some accounts
relate, that before destroying himself he had already sacri-
ficed the life of his daughter. This is not strictly true; he

attempted to kill her, but she shrinking from the blow, escaped with the loss of an arm, and the love of live animated the young princess to seek a refuge from death. The three princes sought to follow her example, but they were less fortunate than their sister. The two younger, while searching for a place of concealment, fell into the power of the tyrant, or, as some assert, of a relation no less cruel. However this may be, both perished. The elder found means to save his life, but we shall see presently that he only prolonged it for a short space beyond that of his brothers, in order to suffer still greater miseries.

Licon, as soon as he found himself master of the capital, took the title of emperor. In order to invest this proceeding with due solemnity, he chose to seat himself on the throne of the Chinese sovereigns ; but it was remarked as an evil omen of the stability of his government that he found it difficult to sit upon, and that he appeared uneasy as if the seat had not been intended for him. His measures for strengthening himself in his new position would have been perfect, if the means he had chosen to bring one Usanguey to his cause had been more successful.

Heroic action of two Chinese. Usanguey had stationed himself in a town on the frontiers of Tartary, whence he watched the motions of the Tartars, who, as he well knew, were not likely to remain long in a state of tranquillity. Licon resolved to march against him with an army of 200,000 men, who only formed a division of his troops, but before resorting to violence he determined to employ artifice. Amongst the grandees of the empire whom the fortune of war had compelled to acknowledge his power, was an old man named Us, the father of the Usanguey of whom we are speaking. When Licon set out on his expedition against the son, he ordered the father to accompany him. Us had no choice when under the commands of a man of Licon's character : he obeyed, and followed the army, in total ignorance of what was required of him. He learnt what it was when he arrived at the spot where the brave Usanguey had entrenched himself to arrest the progress of the tyrant, his troops being too few in number for him to oppose his enemies in the open field. The father was the first instrument which Licon employed in his attack upon the son. He was led under the walls of the town, and the governor was informed that he had been brought there in order to hold a conference with him; but no sooner had Us found himself in the presence of his son, than a message arrived to the latter from Licon, to the effect that he could only hope to save his father's life by immediate submission to the conqueror. Remonstrances and threats added weight to this declaration, and Usanguey was exhorted to submit at once to the yoke which, sooner or later, must be imposed upon him.

Never was a generous heart exposed to such a trial of contending principles as that which overwhelmed Usanguey at this moment. He stood, as it were, between his father and his country, obliged to sacrifice the one or the other, and unable to revenge the death of his sovereign except by consenting to that of his father. He hesitated not, however, and yielding to the dictates of virtue alone, threw himself on his knees, and protested with tears, that though it was not without the most bitter anguish that he consented to witness the death of his parent, in order to save his country, yet the path of duty lay clear before him; and, after all, it was far better for both that one should suffer an honourable death, than that both should live to be despised. If the courage of Usanguey, in this instance, was remarkable, that of Us was still more worthy of admiration; for not only did he refrain from murmuring at his hard fate, but, lauding the patriotism of Usanguey, he submitted to the savage decree of the tyrant with a resolution more akin to the firmness of ancient Rome than to the effeminacy of the Chinese.

This is the account which father Adam's letters give of the transaction; by which it is evident that the father Martini's

3

recollections were not so exact, for he relates that Us showed symptoms of weakness, and entreated his son to submit to the tyrant. The father Adam, who was in the country, and even in the capital, at the time, is the more credible of the two.

It may be easily conceived how this conduct of Usanguey animated the ardour of the soldiers in the defence of their country. Licon would never have been able to resist the sudden outbreak of patriotic feeling that burst forth at this juncture, if he had not had so numerous an army. But the disproportion of numbers was too great; and all that Usanguey could do was to fortify his post, and wait till assistance should arrive. He was reduced to the necessity of asking the aid of strangers, and at the moment he could find none within reach but the Tartars of Niuché, who had for some time apparently been on tolerably good terms with the Chinese. If Usanguey was aware of the danger he invoked in applying for such assistance, the present peril probably appeared to him too pressing to take into consideration one which as yet was only prospective. He therefore despatched a messenger to Zunté, who had succeeded Thienson in the government of Tartary, and whose name had already attained some reputation, and represented to him the straits to which the empire of China was reduced for want of assistance against its own subjects.

The messenger was spared the trouble of calling up his eloquence in order to obtain the object of his mission. Zunté found the dictates of his own ambition more powerful inducements to march against the rebels, than those which the Chinese had made use of to excite his generosity. He mounted his horse, and, placing himself at the head of a fine army, he arrived in time to relieve Usanguey, who still held out with heroic constancy. The rebels soon gave way before the attacks of these able captains. Licon set them the example of flight, and retreated in haste and confusion towards the capital.

The king and the Chinese general pursued them, cutting

to pieces all who ventured to pause in their flight, or who were unable to keep in advance, when a sudden illness, which attacked the king just as they were entering Pekin, arrested the progress of their arms. His death, which followed soon after, threatened to disorganize the undertaking ; but the clear and intelligent instructions which he issued on his death-bed supplied the loss of his personal presence. He had nine brothers, all great military leaders, especially the eldest, called Amavan : feeling his end approaching, he called them into his presence, and having confided to their care his son Chunchi, whom he declared his successor at the age of six years, he exhorted them to carry out an enterprise so glorious to the nation.

The princes, thus left guardians of the youthful monarch, fulfilled the trust committed to them by their sovereign with a fidelity and unanimity which were considered almost miraculous ; and, continuing their march upon Pekin, under the guidance of Usanguey, they compelled Licon to evacuate it The Tartars take posses- as hastily as he had entered it. Usanguey found it no such sion of China. easy matter to dispossess the Tartars when they had once Chunchi is declared emperor. taken possession.

The éclat of such a conquest, and the satisfaction of the people, who looked upon them as their deliverers, and manifested a strong inclination to receive Chunchi as their sovereign, detained them in spite of all Usanguey's efforts to induce them to depart. He spared no exertions in the attainment of this object, but all in vain. The Tartars at first dissembled, their numerical force not being sufficiently strong to enable them to proclaim their intentions ; always replying to Usanguey's representations, that the affairs of China were not in a sufficiently settled state to allow of their leaving it destitute of troops.

It was not long before they expressed themselues more openly. The troops which they had sent orders to levy in Tartary had arrived, upon which they threw off the mask and proclaimed the boy Chunchi emperor of China. This was accomplished with the greater facility, that the father and grandfather of this child, having always projected in their own minds the conquest of this great empire, had taken pains to gain over the mandarins, by the asylum they afforded them at their court, when they were discontented with their government, or were suffering under any injustice.

Usanguey, thus finding himself left unsupported, was compelled to follow in the stream, and submit quietly to what was out of his power to prevent. It was in the year 1644 that Chunchi mounted the throne, and, child as he was, he soon proved himself worthy to reign, by the noble and exalted sentiments which even at this early age distinguished him. A little speech that he made of his own accord to his uncles and his army, won him the affections of his people and excited universal admiration; it was no longer doubted that he was under the special protection of heaven. With a sagacity beyond his years, he decided that he was only half a conqueror, seeing that his possession of the capital did not make him master of the empire. He expressed this opinion to his uncles, who agreed with him, but were highly pleased that his foresight should seem to have excelled theirs.

Licon indeed was still alive and had retreated to Sigan, the capital of the province of Chiensi, where he possessed great resources in troops and money. Chamienchon the other rebel chief reigned in the province of Süchüen; several Princes of the Taimingien House who would have been able to raise a formidable army if there could have existed either concord or subordination among so many of equal rank, had been proclaimed by various parties amongst those Chinese who retained any portion of their national pride.

Usanguey himself was a man to be dreaded, for though the Tartars kept possession of his person, it was essential that they should either attach him to their party or rid themselves of him altogether, and as they respected his valour they were loth to proceed to this extremity.

Fortune favoured the boy-prince, and the talents displayed by Amavan, the eldest of his uncles and his prime-minister, soon overcame all these obstacles. Amavan gained over Usanguey and so completely won his devotion that he entrusted to him without reserve the task of overthrowing Licon, and presented him with the spoils of that chieftain. He vanquished the governor of Süchüen, and after various alternations of success in the war with the Taimingien princes, he beat them one after the other, and at the time of his death left only one unsubdued.

One of these very princes was the cause of the overthrow of the rest, and he was no other than the eldest son of Zonchin whom we have already mentioned. His misfortunes had not yet made life seem unbearable. He had escaped, and had so completely disguised his condition that he hired himself to a Tartar, without any one suspecting his real rank. Those who are born to rule find it hard to accommodate themselves to a life of servitude, and to complete his unhappy lot the young prince found himself in the power of a cruel master. Such a life of hardship soon grew intolerable, he quitted his master and took refuge with an old servant of the emperor his father, believing that the benefits which that prince had conferred upon him must have endeared his memory to him, and that from him he might confidently hope for assistance. He soon found himself mistaken, and he learnt by sad experience that it is vain to look for gratitude when the power of conferring benefits has fled. The ungrateful servant, forgetting all his obligations to so noble a master, compelled the prince to leave his house almost as soon as he had set foot in it, fearing lest he might be discovered, and fearing too lest the vengeance of the conqueror should fall alike on the fugitive and on him who had afforded him shelter.

In this extremity the prince, in despair of finding any place of refuge, resolved to throw himself upon the protection

Adventures of Zonchin's son.

of his maternal grandfather, whom the Tartars had spared and whom they left unmolested, as they did the other mandarins who had submitted to their dominion. He did not find him at home, but in his stead he beheld a person whom he had long believed to be dead. This was the sister whom the emperor, their father, under an impulse of barbarous affection had endeavoured to put to death before destroying himself, though he had only succeeded in cutting off her arm. They recognized one another at the first glance, and in the sudden excitement of this mutual recognition they hastened to embrace one another with a fondness and delight which it is easier to imagine than to describe. They could only speak by their tears, their hearts were overflowing with the tumultuous emotions of joy, sorrow, and affection.

This spectacle, which ought to have touched the heart of the grandfather, who arrived at the moment, awakened in his heart something worse than insensibility. Consulting only the dictates of a hard-hearted policy the unnatural parent refused to acknowledge his grandson and drove him ignominiously from the house. The unhappy prince, now reduced to utter despair and fearful of being discovered, left the capital and went to Nankin. There he learnt that another prince of his house named Hunquan, nephew of Vanlié, had been crowned Emperor of China, and that the heads of the family of Taimin had agreed to support his title. This new freak of fortune caused all his wounds to open afresh. It was far more galling to him to see a subject seated on his throne than a conqueror and an enemy. He could bear it no longer, he proclaimed who he was, and gave proofs of his identity which satisfied all persons except those who had an object in denying it.

It may easily be conceived that Hunquan was not amongst the easiest to convince. As Hunquan had all the power in his own hands, and the prince had asserted his rights too prematurely to give his partizans time to rally round him, he treated him as an impostor, and threw him into prison as a

preliminary step to putting him to death. Those who supported the cause of the prisoner could not submit to see him
whom they regarded as their lawful sovereign the victim of
such treatment. The spirit on either side grew angry, and
a division took place which was of no advantage to any one
but the common enemy. For Amavan, who had made himself master of the province of Chauton, arriving at this juncture on the frontier of that of Nankin, passed it and crossed
the Yellow River without encountering the slightest opposition, after which having occupied all the fortresses on the
north bank of the great river Kian, which the Chinese call
the Son of the Sea, he was met by a formidable resistance at
the passage of this river ; but the brave Hanchouan who de-
fended it having fallen by the hand of one of his own people,
Amavan's path was cleared of all obstacles ; he took Nankin,
and soon after Hunquan, who had fled, was delivered into his
hand by the same traitor who had murdered Hanchouan. He
was carried to Pekin together with his rival, the son of Zonchin, where their opposing claims were decided by the death
of both, a fate which was shared by all who could be found
related to that unhappy house. Father Adam says that at
first the son of Zonchin was spared, whether on account of his
misfortunes, which excited sympathy more than those of his
companions, or that from his doubtful birth he was considered
less formidable. The haughtiness which he evinced even in
prison soon satisfied the incredulous as to his real descent.
As he advanced in years the blood of so many emperors
which flowed in his veins was made evident to himself as well
as to others, and was ultimately the cause that he ruined
himself in the endeavour to make himself feared.

While this bloody tragedy was taking place at Pekin,
against the natural inclinations of the young emperor, which
were always forced by his ministers to give way to political
interests, Amavan was pursuing his successes. He would no
longer have met with any resistance, had not an edict which

Amavan
completes
the con-
quest. His
death. The
emperor
attains his
majority.

he had published, obliging the Chinese to cut off their hair and adopt the Tartar dress, again caused an insurrection against their new rulers. This mark of bondage appeared to them more insupportable than the bondage itself. Too effeminate and cowardly to save their heads, they became brave to save their hair, and had not quarrels broken out amongst those remaining princes of the blood royal who preferred almost equal claims to the throne, the Tartars would have run the risk of losing their conquests instead of increasing them. But these divisions enabled Amavan to ruin some by means of the others, and he ended by exterminating them all, after which he returned to Pekin, and thither he carried his laurels only to hide them in the grave, for he died in 1651, soon after his return, leaving the emperor, who was now fourteen years old, and was married to the daughter of the king of Tanyu, competent to assume the reins of government in compliance with the wishes of his people.

Religion preserved during the revolution.

The Christian religion suffered much by the fall of the Chinese princes, especially by the death of one named Yunlié, who lived for some years after Amavan had wrested from him the possession of Canton, the capital of the province, where he had been proclaimed king; but his party, too weak to retrieve its losses, had been compelled to abandon him to his fate. Services which had been rendered him by two Christian mandarins, and the circumstance of his chief minister being a Christian likewise, had made him favourable to the cause of Christianity, so that a Jesuit, named Father Cofler, who was attached to that court, had made many converts. The prince himself was not far from the kingdom of heaven, his wife and his son were baptised by the names of Helen and Constantine, and he had sent another Jesuit to Rome to give in his allegiance to the vicar of Jesus Christ. All this was put a stop to by the defeat of Yunlié. Constantine met with the same fate as his father; the queen was taken to Pekin, where she still lives, and where it is said that the loss of her liberty has by no means affected her faith; the remainder were dispersed, and this unhappy Church was left in a mournful state of desolation.

While the cause of religion was suffering these defeats, it obtained full compensation by the cordial reception given by the conquerors to the ministers of the Gospel. The Jesuits were at the time scattered over the whole of China, and they had several churches. Some, indeed, had been buried in the ruins of the cities where they lived, not one of them having abandoned his flock; but the majority of them were very well treated by the Tartars. A few of them had adventures worthy of record.

Father Martini, to whom Europe is indebted for the greater part of her knowledge of Chinese history, relates of himself, that after an expedition he had made from Mancheu, capital of the province, to Venchui, which lies close by, it was suddenly noised abroad that the Tartars were at hand; and the rumour was only too correct. The father lodged in a large house, in which several persons hastily took refuge with him, hoping by this means to save their lives, or to encourage one another to support their approaching fate. He received them with a kindness which deserved that the blessing of heaven should accompany the exertions he made to save them. As soon as he learnt that the Tartars were about to enter the town, he put up on the door of his house an inscription in these words: "Here resides a doctor of the divine law, come from the Great West." In the vestibule he placed a number of tables covered with books, telescopes, burning-glasses, and similar articles, which excite great admiration and respect in those countries. In the middle of it all he erected an altar, and placed upon it an image of the Saviour. This spectacle was attended with all the effect which he anticipated. The Tartars were much impressed, and far from injuring any one, their chief sent for the father, received him very favourably, and, unwilling to compel him

4

to forsake the national dress, he asked him frankly if he had any objection to having his hair cut off. As the father made no opposition the captain had it cut off in his presence; and when the father observed to him laughingly, that the Chinese dress which he still wore did not suit with his shorn head, the Tartar took off his own boots and cap and made him put them on; and after entertaining him at his own table, he sent him back to his church with letters and passports, which effectually protected him and his fellow-Christians from the insults of the soldiery.

A still more singular history is that of the father des Magalhans, the author of the well-written and curious observations, to which the embellishments of the learned abbé Bernou have added a fresh interest. He and father Buglio were with the army of Chamienchon, who had taken a fancy to them, and who had promised that at the conclusion of the war he would build a magnificent temple to the God of the Christians. It was a mission which at first was not displeasing to them, for they found much to do, and still more to encourage their hopes in the propagation of the true faith. But as time advanced their position became quite unendurable. Chamienchon proved to be one of the most cruel and sanguinary monsters that ever existed. The inhuman atrocities of which he was guilty would be perfectly incredible, if they had not been related by such trustworthy witnesses. If he happened to find in the street a person who had offended him, the provocation was sufficient for him to destroy all its inhabitants.

A fault committed by a single bonze, was atoned for by the blood of 20,000 persons; for the error of one soldier a whole legion suffered the same fate. One day he put to the sword all the inhabitants of a certain town, which numbered a population of 600,000 souls; on another occasion he ordered his soldiers to kill all their wives, and he set them the example by only sparing twenty out of the three hundred which he himself possessed. If the simple perusal of these crimes fills the mind with horror, it may be inferred what were the feelings of those who were compelled to witness them. They could bear it at last no longer, and they resolved to leave this savage or to attempt to humanize him. They began by respectfully remonstrating with him; their language then grew a little more emphatic, but, finding all their attempts useless, and unable to endure any longer the sight of so much human blood shed by the commands of this merciless wretch, they frankly asked permission to withdraw from the army. Nothing more was required to rouse all the fury of this wild beast, and to convert his friendship into deadly hatred. He condemned them to death, and they were about to be hewn in pieces, when the son of the tyrant, who had grown attached to them, persuaded him to suspend this bloody tragedy for a short time. But he was none the less resolved upon their destruction, and on a certain day he had caused the priests to be led before him that he might preside at the execution of the sentence, when, at the critical moment, intelligence was brought to him that the Tartar army, from which he fancied himself quite secure, was ready to fall upon him. He sprang upon his horse without waiting to put on his armour, and encountered at the gates of his camp the vanguard of the army, one of whom discharged an arrow against him with so true an aim that he fell dead, and thus the human race was delivered from the greatest enemy it ever had. The tyrant's death was followed by the flight of his army; those who escaped destruction at the hands of the Tartars were completely dispersed.

The fathers were saved from this danger only to fall into another. For having taken the resolution of presenting themselves before the Tartar general, they were met in the vicinity of the camp by one of the outposts, who not understanding their language, and taking them for spies, attacked them, wounded them with their arrows, and left them on the ground for dead. They narrowly escaped this fate, for they were both severely wounded, and father Buglio was pierced by a javelin, which neither he nor his companion were able to extract. By the greatest good fortune, as the father de Magalhans was searching for something to enable him to draw out the iron, he found a pair of pincers, with which he succeeded in extracting it. While these two fathers were thus endeavouring to relieve one another's sufferings, their wounds being already bandaged, and as they were deliberating as to the course they should pursue in their present situation, they saw advancing towards them another squadron of Tartars, much more numerous than the former.

The treatment they had just received did not augur well for their present chances of safety; but they were agreeably surprised when the leader of the troop, who was the Tartar general, having heard of the disaster that had befallen them, and conjecturing who they might be, accosted them civilly, expressed his regret as to their adventure, and conducted them to his camp. Nothing could equal the attention he paid them. He provided them with everything they could require, caused their wounds to be dressed every day, and as soon as they had recovered, he accompanied them to Pekin, where they found the celebrated father Adam Schall in high favour with the emperor: and they rightly attributed to his influence all the civilities they had received, and which were extended to their brethren all over the kingdom.

Father Adam Schall. His favour with the emperor. The father Adam Schall was a German Jesuit, a native of Cologne, who having visited China as a missionary in the first instance, and having been sent to Pekin to learn the Chinese sciences, had acquired such a reputation at the court of the emperor Zonchin by his knowledge of mathematics, that he was regarded as one of the first men in the empire. As he remained at Pekin through all the revolutions, which in so short a space of time had so repeatedly changed the aspect of the monarchy, he was exposed to a thousand dangers; but when this change of government took place, he had the good fortune to find that he enjoyed as much consideration in the Tartar court as he had received in that of the Chinese prince. Amavan contracted a friendship with him and paid him several visits, and finding in him not only great scientific attainments but much merit and virtue, presented him to the young emperor.

The youth of this prince did not prevent him from deriving great satisfaction from the society of the father, and he pressed him to repeat his visits. It is impossible to say how far this intercourse contributed to form the intellect and the heart of Chunchi: both were naturally of a high order, but that which by nature was good in him, became excellent by education. Accordingly all the chief men of the empire were so impatient that he should assume the reins of government, that one of his uncles, having intrigued to obtained the post which the death of Amavan had left vacant, and to retain the young king in a state of tutelage for some time longer, he excited a general opposition amongst the courtiers; they brought to the palace the insignia of their various offices, and protested that they would not resume them till the emperor should undertake the government of his people.

The prince not daring to carry his pretensions and his intrigues any farther, the emperor assumed the government, Chunchi the Elder: his great qualities. and appeared all at once so well skilled in the art of reigning that he excited general admiration and won the hearts of all his subjects. He possessed not only a high order of intellect, but a singular aptitude for everything. He gave his orders in the field as if he had grown grey in harness. He kept a watchful eye on the conduct of the magistrates and the officers of the crown, in consequence of which nothing escaped his penetration, and though he was in general inclined to gentle measures in his dealings with his subjects he rather erred on the side of severity when it was a question of punishing any misdemeanour of a public functionary. Having been informed

one day that those who presided at the examination of the
candidates for the doctorate, which is necessary for all those
who aspire to any of the higher offices in the state, had winked
at the ignorance of some amongst the number to whom they
had sold their votes, he obliged these latter to undergo a second
examination, and condemned to death thirty-six of the examiners, upon the plea that those who sold justice were capable of
betraying their country. The policy he pursued in order to
pacify his dominions, after the turmoil of his conquest had
subsided, was to amalgamate so completely the Chinese and
Tartar races that they should by degrees merge into one nation. It was to carry out this principle that he placed an
equal number of both in all the tribunals, and that in the administration of the government he employed the services of
both indiscriminately, when he found them equally deserving
of his confidence. In the same way as he had caused the
Chinese to adopt the Tartar dress, he introduced the regula-
tions of the Chinese police amongst his Tartars as being more
sagacious and better conceived. He confirmed the privileges
which the laws of China had granted for the encouragement
of literature, but he took every precaution to prevent the
national warlike character from degenerating under its influence, as it had done under the late reigns, being desirous of
introducing a martial spirit into the Chinese philosophy by
the infusion of Tartar discipline and courage. Thus he
brought to a successful termination all those wars which Ama-
yan had left unfinished, of which the most formidable was
that which he conducted against Icoan, or rather against his
children.

Story of a
man of for-
tune named
Icoan, and
of his son
Quesin.   Icoan, otherwise known as Chinchilon, was born in the
province of Fokien and had been compelled by poverty to
abandon his native country at a very early age. He came
to Macao, where he succeeded in bettering his condition, and
having been instructed in the rudiments of the Christian religion he received the rite of baptism. His godfather, who

was a rich Portuguese, grew so fond of him that when he died he left him heir to a portion of his property. Possessed of this capital he engaged in trade, in which he was successful, and proved himself so skilful that in a short time he became one of the most celebrated and the richest merchant of the Indies. He soon found himself the owner of vessels, and his ambition having kept pace with his wealth he began to adopt the manners and mode of life of the great nobles. His opulence won him friends, but it likewise raised him up enemies, who made every effort to prejudice the emperor Zonchin against him. This prince was however just beginning to find himself too much beset with enemies to think of creating a new one, and instead of heeding the complaints which poured into his ears he resolved to attach him to his interests by giving him the appointment of admiral in the Chinese seas. Icoan was not ungrateful for this mark of favour; for hearing that the tyrant Licon had levied war upon the emperor he assembled his troops to hasten to his assistance. His fidelity was of no avail to the unhappy Zonchin, and he received the news of his fate as he was marching to his aid. Seeing therefore that there remained nothing more to be done in the service of his prince and of his country, he retraced his steps, resolving to pursue his labours for his own aggrandizement, and to take advantage of the public ruin which he could not avert to advance his own interests which were already in a flourishing state.

In truth the commotions in the empire tended to increase his own importance, especially since Quesin, his son, whose character resembled his own, was old enough to assist him. They both attached themselves to the cause of one of the Taimingien princes, who had claimed the sovereignty. They maintained him on the throne for a considerable time, and would have upheld him altogether if he had helped himself in the smallest degree. As for them, as they could perfectly subsist without him, they made no scruple of deserting him when they found that his cause was hopeless ; and continuing the contest on their own account, they became so formidable that the Tartars eagerly sought their alliance, and made them the most splendid offers upon the condition that they would submit to their authority. Quesin firmly resisted, but Icoan was more easily persuaded, and, against the urgent advice of his son, he imprudently surrendered himself to the victors.

The ministers thought themselves secure of the son as soon as the father was in their power, never doubting that the parent would employ every argument to win over his son. Consequently they began by treating Icoan with all respect, making his position as agreeable as possible to him ; but they changed their tone when they discovered that it was labour thrown away, and that Quesin remained as obstinate as ever. At first they took from him all his appointments, and ended by reducing him to such a state of destitution, that he subsisted for a considerable time upon the charity of the Jesuits of Pekin, whom he had always protected, though the ambition which had engrossed all his thoughts had left him but an indifferent Christian. Poverty was soon followed by exile and imprisonment, and finally a violent death terminated his misfortunes and his life.

Quesin, who cherished towards his father all those sentiments of filial devotion which Chinese morality inculcates, made every effort to revenge his death ; and it was in the war which he prosecuted with this motive that the young prince, at the moment of attaining his majority, found himself involved. Quesin had remained with his vessels, and had contented himself with the sovereignty of the seas, where, by means of the powerful naval force under his command he had established a superiority which was the terror of the neighbouring coasts. He placed such confidence in his soldiers, that as soon as he heard of the death of his father, he resolved upon obtaining retribution. The emperor was prepared, and lost no time in sending reinforcements to the maritime provinces, and placing tried officers in the fortified towns. Fortunately, he had entrusted the defence of Nankin to two officers, who would counterbalance one another by their opposite dispositions to gentleness and severity. For Quesin having presumed to attack this large town, the Tartar captain who commanded the garrison proposed to massacre all the burghers: their numbers, he urged, were too great for any order to be maintained amongst them, even should the siege be protracted. The Chinese magistrate Lam, who presided over the civil tribunals, was horrified by the proposal, and vehemently opposed such a barbarous intention. " If you intend to carry this measure into execution," he said boldly to the Tartar, " you must begin with me." These words recalled this violent and sanguinary chieftain to his senses, and he soon after acknowledged, that it was possible to obtain a more glorious victory over the enemy, than by staining it with cruelty. The siege had lasted three weeks, and the town was beginning to suffer, when the besiegers conceived the idea of celebrating the birthday of their general by a magnificent feast. They gave themselves up to every kind of excess on this occasion. Having abandoned themselves during a whole day to wine, and the following night to slumber, they were attacked by the besieged, who had discovered their powerless condition. Three thousand were left dead on the field, and the rest were compelled to take refuge in their ships.

Quesin learnt experience from his defeat, and was careful to select a better field for his operations. He remained at sea, and defeated the imperial fleets in several engagements. In one of these, having taken prisoners three thousand Tartars, he had their noses cut off and sent them back to Pekin, where the emperor, who always punished public faults with merciless severity, condemned them all to death, saying that they ought to have sought it in battle, and to have preferred it to a disgrace which was reflected upon the nation.

If Quesin knew how to maintain himself at sea, the emperor, on the other hand, made himself quite inaccessible on land, and was so successful that the enemy was obliged to retire elsewhere with his forces. Quesin had long meditated the conquest of the Island of Formosa, then occupied by the Dutch. He determined to attack them, and was moreover bold enough to make this resolution at a time when they had made an alliance with the Tartars against him. In spite of these two formidable powers, he took possession of the island, and caused himself to be proclaimed king. Not content with this, he even attempted to exact a tribute from the Spaniards of the Philippines, and sent an ambassador to Manilla to demand it. His power was sufficiently established to have ensured compliance with this demand, had not quarrels arisen in his family. It happened that he had left his wives, together with one of his sons named Chius, in an island in the province of Fokien, where his own father had built a fortress. This son, forgetting all proper respect to his father, had become enamoured of one of his wives, and unfortunately he had not found her insensible to his passion. This insult excited the indignation of Quesin to such a degree, that he resolved that his son should atone for it with his life. The young man was warned of this determination, and, with the assistance of his mother, who lived in the same fortress and was a woman of superior intellect, he entered into a treaty with the Tartars, forestalling thereby the arrival of the messenger whom his father had sent to put him to death. No sooner had he taken this step, however, than he heard that the revolt had produced such an effect upon Quesin's mind that it had caused his death. This event retarded for some time the reduction of the Island of Formosa, and it was not destined to be accomplished, as we shall see, till the reign of the present emperor.

The greatness of Chunchi manifested itself not only in his wars and conquests, but it was conspicuous also amidst the splendour of his court, where he supported the dignity of the empire, and asserted over the neighbouring princes an air of superiority which few cared to dispute. The king of Corea visiting Pekin, made his court to him like a private subject. Father Adam says that he saw him there, and conversed with him frequently. Ambassadors flocked thither from all countries, and it was in his reign that the Dutch sent their famous mission, the account of which is found in the admirable collection of curious narratives and voyages which M. Thevenot has laid before the public. The Muscovites also sent one which did not prove satisfactory, as they claimed greater honours than the emperor thought consistent with his dignity to allow them.

Chunchi was as amiable in private life and amongst those who had the privilege of knowing him personally, as he was distinguished in his public capacity. The terms on which he lived with father Adam, even after he had attained his majority, entirely bears out this assertion. The young emperor used to call him *mafa*, a name which corresponds to that of father in our language ; and, in truth, he felt towards him all the affection of a son. Indeed, he rather oppressed him with favours, by insisting, against his desire, that he should accept the post of chief professor of mathematics, which is one of the first offices in the state. It was the only occasion on which the father found himself in danger of forfeiting the good will of his sovereign towards himself and the other ministers of religion. In all their other relations, it was father Adam's opinion that he knew no one so pleasant to live with as Chunchi. No one ever had cause to tremble from the fear of incurring his displeasure, by some of those trifling accidents which so often occur to trouble the serenity of men in power. The father never found it necessary to consult his whims or to humour his fancies. The emperor

Chunchi in private life.

took everything from the father in good part, and it was remarked with pleasure, that though his temper was naturally
warm and hasty, he never varied in his conduct towards his
friend.

Chunchi placed the most boundless confidence in his honesty, and was so well assured of his affection that he always
listened patiently to the frequent and severe rebukes which
this faithful servant administered to him, though they might
condemn many of his pleasures; and even if he did not invariably reform his conduct, he had the candour to confess that
he would have done better to follow his advice. The grandees, who saw what a powerful influence father Adam exerted
over the mind of the prince, often employed him to commu-
nicate what they had not the courage to say themselves.

It so happened that a rumour had been circulated highly
injurious to the reputation of the emperor, and the courtiers
industriously propagated it, in order to create a scandal. No
one dared to inform the principal person concerned in the
affair, and the father was the only person who could be induced to undertake it. He requested an audience, and throw-
ing himself at his feet, his eyes full of tears, he put a paper
into his hand which acquainted him with the scandalous stories
that were afloat in connexion with his name. The emperor
read it, and coloured as he did so; but he did not appear
offended, and only said, as he raised his aged councillor, that
the whole affair was very much exaggerated.

Another time the emperor was so completely overwhelmed
with grief at the loss of one of his wives, to whom he was de-
votedly attached, that he sank into a state of complete apathy,
and entirely neglected all his affairs. As no one would venture to address him, the ministers, who were exceedingly
embarrassed respecting the decision of several matters which
required the sovereign's attention, were at a loss what course
to pursue. Father Adam relieved them from their perplex-
ity. He made his way to the emperor's presence, and gently

and respectfully represented to him how much he lowered himself in the public estimation by his present conduct. Father Adam knew how to work upon his peculiar disposition, and he soon brought him to see the wisdom of his exhortations. The emperor was so grateful to him for the interest he took in his welfare, that he wrote to him on the following day a letter full of expressions of the warmest affection, while he conjured him to continue towards himself a friendship so valuable to his person and the state.

One day the father feared that he had offended him by a similar proceeding on his part,—on which occasion he had certainly expressed himself rather strongly. The emperor had asked him how it was that the persons he employed in the management of the public affairs performed their duty so negligently at times, since he treated them so kindly, and never harrassed or tormented them. " It ought not to astonish you so much, sire," replied the father, " it does occasionally happen that your majesty somewhat sets them the example." The emperor made no reply to this explanation, and the father thought he was offended ; but he was surprised to find that, after a few moments, the emperor began to talk to him again just as usual, and with no alteration of manner.

On another occasion, after he had been sitting for some time with the father, in his own room, he went down into the garden with him to see a forge for the manufacture of mathematical instruments. The workmen retired when they saw the emperor ; but he desired them to go on with their work, and stood near to watch them. At last he got so close to them that when they began to strike the glowing iron the sparks reached him. He stepped back, but in doing so he came upon a ditch covered with loose planks ; one of these gave way, and he narrowly escaped falling into it. Father Adam shuddered with apprehension lest the prince should look upon this accident as a bad omen, as it had occurred on the eve of his birthday,—a day on which every event is carefully noted down by the superstitious astrologers of China. He fell on his knees, and asked the emperor's pardon for the danger to which his majesty had been exposed through his imprudence, conjuring him not to draw any evil augury from an accident which was purely fortuitous. The emperor smiled on hearing these words, and, kindly raising father Adam, he said, " Go, mafa, there are few men in this world who do not occasionally make a false step."

He excited the admiration of all those who recollected the haughty and exclusive manners of the late Chinese sovereigns, by his easy familiarity with this foreigner. Not only did he give him free access to his palace, but he often went to visit him, and used to spend several hours with him. It is a custom in China that when once a seat has been occupied by the emperor, no one else is ever allowed to sit upon it, and it is covered with a yellow cloth,—the imperial colour. As Chunchi always sat down on whatever seat happened to be nearest to him, the father said to him one day, smiling, " But where does your majesty intend me to sit henceforward?"

" Wherever you like," replied the emperor; " we do not stand upon ceremony, you and I."

Their discussions together were on various subjects: mathematics, morality, and religion,—for the father had the art of leading the conversation from agreeable to useful subjects, and as much as possible to those which might open his eyes to the truths of the gospel. One of these conversations is related at full length in the memoirs which remain to us of father Adam. It shows so clearly the penetration and honesty of the emperor whose history we are recording, that we cannot do better than repeat it here.

Conversation with father Adam on the subject of religion.

In the year 1656, the emperor having desired the father to come and meet him in a park where he was hunting; the father accordingly came, and as soon as the hunting was over the following discussion took place on the subject of a book on astronomy, which he had presented to him.

"I have heard it said," began the prince, "that certain conjunctions of the stars portend certain events. If this be true, as the course of the stars is regulated, our destinies must be ruled also, and it is useless to take measures to avert that which is inevitable."

Father Adam, who occasionally took advantage of the emperor's curiosity in observing the stars, to teach him to fear Him who reigns supreme over them, replied, "Sire, far above all the stars there is One who has created them, One who often makes use of them to warn us men, and more particularly the princes of the earth, of the sins which displease Him, by the chastisements with which He threatens them. But this same God, who governs the stars, and makes use of the constellations as warnings to men, has given them free will to escape from the punishments with which they are threatened, by a timely repentance."

"Can you tell me," replied the emperor, "who is this God of whom you so often speak to me?"

"He is an invisible God," answered the father; "but He reveals himself to man in His works. He it is who created the heavens, and who governs the various motions that we admire in that starry host; and this is why we Christians call him by the name of Creator, or Lord.

"I will grant you that much," replied the emperor, returning to the point; "but I recollect your often telling me that those warnings we were speaking of just now apply more particularly to me. Why to me more than other kings?"

"Your majesty," said the father with great presence of mind, "has assumed, amongst other titles, that of 'son of heaven'; you cannot then wonder that the God of heaven watches over you more than over others."

"But," resumed the emperor, "if I were to correct myself of the faults which you have pointed out to me, would that be sufficient to ward off the chastisements with which you threaten me?"

" I cannot doubt it, sire. You would not, indeed, attain the power of changing the course of the stars, and their conjunctions in the heavens; but we have a proverb in Europe, which says that a wise man has dominion over the heavenly bodies."

" Pray, mafa," rejoined the emperor, " tell me the best way to correct my faults."

" I have often taken advantage of the liberty your majesty allows me, to tell you freely my opinion of your conduct. You will have made a great improvement when you have learnt to temper justice with mercy, for your notions of justice too often degenerate into harshness and cruelty; when you have more consideration for those who are about your person, by letting them receive occasionally some token of your approbation and liberality; when you apply yourself more assiduously to promote the welfare of your people, and increase their happiness;—in a word, when your majesty, loving God, our common Father, above all things, will have learnt to feel the same compassion for the sorrows of your fellow men, who by nature are your brothers, as you would wish them to feel for you, if you were in their place,—according to that other precept of right reason, that we must do unto others as we would they should do unto us."

When the father had reached this point, the emperor argued, that princes who are accustomed to look down upon all men as their inferiors, are not willing to acknowledge this law of equality: he even confessed that he could not conceive it, a remark which led the father to explain to him the Decalogue.

The emperor listened to his disquisition, which was tolerably long, without interrupting him, and was struck with admiration at so perfect a code of laws.

" Mafa," he answered, " have you many disciples in this country, who observe all these precepts which you have been explaining to me ?"

" We have rather a considerable number," answered the father, " and if some of them forsake their duty occasionally, it is because we are not supported here by the civil' authority as we are in Europe, where we can punish those who violate the law."

" But how do you mean," replied the emperor, " are kings in your country subject to this law as much as ordinary people ?"

" Much more so," rejoined the father, " for kings ought to set a good example to their subjects."

" What ! does that apply to me as well, even though I am not yet a Christian ?"

" This law, sir, is obligatory upon all men, and all are obliged to obey it under the pain of eternal punishment."

" That requires great strength," said the emperor, " and how is it to be obtained ?"

" God gives us strength," answered the father, " and it never fails us when we need it : with this help all difficulties can be overcome, and it is only necessary to have the will."

" You have convinced me," was the emperor's conclusion, " and it seems to me that I may hope to accomplish what so many others have done ; and I *will* do it, I am quite determined."

Having arrived at this satisfactory result, the emperor turned the conversation to the subject of the Zonchin, his predecessor, and asked the father what was the cause of his fall.

The father answered, that he was an extremely well-disposed prince, moral, careful of the welfare of his people, but that he had too much confidence in himself and his own judgment ; while his blind attachment to unfaithful magistrates and soldiers had been the cause of his ruin. He added, in order to excite the emulation of the emperor by a noble example, that this prince respected the divine law ; and that, if the blow which destroyed him had not fallen so unexpectedly, he would very likely have embraced Christianity.

By such conferences as the above, father Adam so conciliated the young conqueror to the Christian religion, that he constantly favoured the same, and accorded to its preachers full liberty for its diffusion. Chunchi afforded every hope that he would shortly profess it, but the same passion which caused Solomon to embrace the false gods, which he knew not, led Chunchi to desert the true God, who had been brought to his knowledge.

Among the women of rank at the court of the empress, was one of whom the prince became desperately enamoured. His passion became too violent for long suppression: he disclosed it to its object one day, as she was leaving the imperial apartment, and omitted no argument to obtain her acquiescence. He met, as he expected, with resistance ; but, from the manner of her reply, he judged that her severity would not be invincible. This lady was married to a young Tartar of very good family, to whom, either from artifice or simplicity, she confided the circumstance of the emperor's passion, and even the details of the conversation above mentioned. The Tartar was not satisfied with the manner in which she had spoken, and not considering that she had repulsed the attack with sufficient vivacity, gave her instructions for the next similar occasion. The lady was as simple, or as subtle, with the emperor, as she had been with her husband ; for she communicated to the emperor the lesson she had received, and gave him to understand that her resistance was due to conjugal obedience, and not, as it ought to have been, to virtue and fidelity.

The emperor, no longer under the control of reason, was so irritated on meeting with this obstacle to his desires, that he sent for the unhappy husband and sought a quarrel with him on the pretext of some maladministration of his charge, and became so excited in the discussion as to strike him.

The Tartar scarcely survived this indignity; mortification carried him to the grave within three days from the occurrence.

His decease gave much pleasure to his rival, and apparently little distress to his widow, for the emperor married her incontinently and declared her his queen. To crown his felicity, she bore him a son, but this was the last fruit of this fatal marriage. The child died soon after birth, and was shortly followed by its mother.

It is easy to conceive the emperor's affliction, but scarcely so to imagine the excesses to which he was led by his sorrow. Great difficulty was found in preventing him from suicide, and the empress mother had to throw herself upon him to snatch away the sword with which he was about to execute his purpose. He so far forgot on this occasion, not only his virtue, but the common rules of humanity, that he revived, in favour of his deceased queen, the barbarous Tartar custom, abolished by Chinese civilization, which compels the officers and slaves of persons of rank to follow them to the tomb, in order to render to them in the next world the services they had performed towards them in this. Upwards of thirty persons died by their own hand in virtue of this order of the emperor.

The greatest evil of all was, that this princess, being extremely addicted to idol worship and to the superstition of the bonzes, had on this point corrupted the mind of the emperor, especially by a solemn testamentary request, that he would cause these priests to celebrate certain idolatrous rites on her behalf. For the unhappy prince having executed but too faithfully this disposition, became thereby so habituated to Pagan superstition, that it became impossible for father Adam to revive in him the good sentiments he had previously entertained towards the true faith. That apostolic man omitted nothing which could tend to cure the blindness of the prince. He often represented to him, with warmth and force, the injury which kings, who had abandoned themselves to their passions and to superstition, had inflicted on their states. He dwelt especially on the infinite mischiefs which they incur by their love for women, the excesses to which it leads them, the contempt into which they fall by the neglect of public affairs, the indifference to the public good, the insensibility towards the glory and interest of the state which this passion naturally produces. The emperor did not resent these remonstrances of father Adam, which he received as proofs of his attachment, but neither did he profit by them. " I pardon," he would often say in defending himself, " in acknowledgement of your zeal for my person, your invectives against my conduct ; but, after all, mafa, is it so bad as you describe it ? Can you, religious man as you are, gainsay my acts of obedience to my own religion ? Would you not censure me for obstructing you in acts of obedience to your own ? Why desire to prevent my practice of mine ?"

Death of
Chunchi.
Against such obduracy, the father saw well that he had no further resource but tears and prayers. The emperor, however, falling sick of the small-pox, which carried him off in five days, father Adam tried a last effort. He was received, as usual, with every demonstration of good will, but he left the dying prince with as little hope as ever of his conversion. The prince, nevertheless, after the father had retired, appeared to fall back into a firmer state of mind, and was heard to recall to recollection passages of the conversation of his faithful adviser. He exhibited repentance for his excesses, and censured them in the hearing of those about him. He put order to the affairs of his empire, declaring his son Cambi, a boy of only eight years old, his successor, and naming four principal officers of the crown as his guardians. After which, having arrayed himself in the imperial vestments, and bidding adieu to his attendants, he expired, at the age of twenty-four. A monarch worthy of a better fate,

if his natural good qualities be considered, but deserving also such a chastisement, if we regard his abuse of the grace which heaven had shewn him.

The queen, his mother, after his example, renewed the cruel custom of compelling the living to follow the dead. Chunchi had had a favourite, a young Tartar, one of the best born and best bred adherents of the courts. As soon as the emperor had expired, the empress sent for this young man, and looking at him with an eye of anger, said : " Is it possible that you are still alive?" The prince understood this language, and the empress was not long in making it clear. " Go," she said, more gently, " go and keep company with my son. He loved you well, and, as I believe, you replied to his affection and the honour of his friendship. He expects you; go and rejoin him, and by your promptitude in so doing shew yourself worthy of his impatience for the meeting. You love him. Further discourse is needless. Go and bid adieu to your parents, but hasten to shew your fidelity to your sovereign and your attachment to your friend." The sorrow which this sentence, so sad and so little expected, caused to the young man's family, is not to be described. He himself quitted life with regret, for his attachment was not strong enough to make him hate existence. He was counselled to escape, and was not deaf to the advice; but the queen took care to anticipate it, for she sent him in a gilded casket a bow-string by two messengers, who were charged to give every assistance for its use, which any failure of his own courage might render necessary. Thus perished this prince, happy had he been less favoured by nature and fortune.

The Christian religion and its preachers appeared to have lost everything by the death of Chunchi. For, albeit, for some time things remained in their former state, and the four regents even conferred on father Adam the title of preceptor to the young emperor, a cabal of bonzes and Mahometans, *Persecutian of the Chris- tians. Death of father Adam.*

animated by a certain Yam-quam-sien, a man as barbarous
as his name, excited such a tempest against Christianity as to
result in an attempt at its extermination. All its preachers
having been summoned to Pekin, were loaded with chains,
and, with the exception of two or three whom the young
emperor chose to retain, were all exiled to Canton. Christians were persecuted in various ways, and five mandarins
glorified their profession by martyrdom.

Death of
father
Adam.

It was at this crisis that father Adam shewed himself that
apostolic follower of St. Paul, who knew how to use riches
and poverty, good fortune and bad, repute and infamy alike,
to the advancement of God's glory. Fallen from fame, deprived of his dignities, loaded with reproach and calumny,
he endured imprisonment and fetters, and was finally condemned to death for having preached the faith of Christ;
shewing by his constancy that he considered himself even
more happy to confess that name in a dungeon than to have
preached it with honour in a palace. His sentence was not
executed, but age and suffering soon performed the office of
the executioner; for, soon after his deliverance from prison,
God completed it, by dismissing him from the bondage of the
flesh to enjoy the perfect liberty of the children of heaven.

China owes to the prudent zeal of this great man, the
consecration and the diffusion of the true faith among her
people. As he had accepted with this view alone the charge
with which he had been honoured by the emperor, he enjoyed it only so far as he thought conducive to that end.
He had reduced, in its discharge, all he could of the pomp
of Chinese ceremonial, retaining so much only as he could
not retrench without degrading his office, and forfeiting the
advantage derivable from it for the advancement of the faith.
The honours of the mandarinat did not diminish in him
the charity of the apostle. The entire court admired in him
the readiness of one, who conversed so familiarly with one of
the greatest monarchs in the world, to converse with the

poorest, to visit the most wretched when they had need of him. He had the courage to expose himself to the plague, to succour a family afflicted with it, and among them people who had endeavoured to do him injury. He contracted the disease, and only escaped from it because God reserved him for the glorious departure, in which he crowned great labours by great sufferings, and by a glorious confession of the gospel which he announced.

THE HISTORY

TARTAR CONQUERORS WHO SUBDUED
CHINA.

BOOK THE SECOND.

Camhi the Second, conqueror of China. His qualities. GOD had too great designs in elevating to the throne of China Camhi, who occupies it at present, not to endow him with all those qualities which could form a great emperor. He has a solid intellect, with great reasoning powers, a lively and sagacious intelligence, better adapted and disposed to the cultivation of literature than the late emperor his father. With all this he is brave, wise, and politic, while his straightforward character would do honour to a Christian prince.

He gave proofs of his excellent heart as soon as he had mounted the throne. He had been brought up in a separate house with his mother, who had the charge of him. He had no sooner been taken to the palace, than he summoned all the children of his own age who had been his companions in his maternal home, and formed for himself a juvenile court. When he was fourteen years old, he took the reins of government into his own hands and soon let it be seen that princes do not always require the aid of experience and age to make them worthy to reign. Even at this early age, traits are related of him which stamp him as a hero. Here are two, by which we may judge of the rest. One day, as he was passing by a sepulchre, which he thought neglected and ill-adorned, he inquired whose it was; those who were about him having answered that it was the sepulchre of Zonchin, the last king of China of the Taimingien race, he knelt down, and striking his forehead upon the earth to testify the respect he felt for the memory of this unfortunate emperor, he lifted up his voice weeping, and said these words, interrupted by the sobs which a heartfelt compassion wrung from him: "Pardon me thy misfortunes, Zonchin. After all I was not the cause of them. They were thy subjects who betrayed thee, and the violent acts of thy ministers, which compelled thy servants to summon us to their assistance."

After these words he burnt some perfumes over the tomb, and ordered that the very next day a superb mausoleum should be begun, and set apart the necessary sums for the expenses of the erection.

Another time that he was out hunting, he got separated from his suite, and he met an old man who was weeping bitterly, and appeared to be overcome by some very violent affliction. He approached him, touched by the state in which he saw him, and without discovering himself asked him what was the matter.

"The matter," answered the old man, " alas, my lord, if I were to tell you, it is an evil to which you could apply no remedy."

"Perhaps, my good man," replied the emperor, "I might be able to give you more assistance than you think; so confide to me what it is that afflicts you."

"If you *will* know," answered the man, "it is that the superintendent of one of the pleasure-houses of the emperor, finding that my property, which is close to the royal abode, suits his convenience, has taken possession of it, and has reduced me to the state of beggary in which you see me. He has done more; I had an only son, who was the support

7

of my old age : he has taken him from me and has made him his slave.   There, my lord, is the reason why I weep."

The emperor was so touched by this narrative, that, only bent upon punishing a crime which was committed in his name, he first of all inquired of the old man if it was far off from where they stood to the house of which he was speaking ; and the old man having answered that the distance was barely a mile and a half, he told him that he would go with him to the spot to urge the superintendent to restore to him his property and his son, and that he did not despair of being able to persuade him.

" Persuade him !" rejoined the old man, " ah, my lord, remember, if you please, that I have just informed you that this man belongs to the emperor.   It is not safe for you or for me to go and make such a proposition to him; he would only treat me more cruelly, and you would suffer some insult, to which I beg you will not expose yourself."

" Do not be uneasy about that," replied the emperor, " I have made up my mind to everything ; but I will go, and I hope our negociation will be more successful than you imagine."

The old man, who saw in this unknown something of that glory which high birth stamps upon the forehead of men of his rank, thought he had better not refuse any longer.   He only objected, that being feeble with age and on foot, he should not be able to keep up with the horse on which the emperor was mounted.

" I am young," answered the prince, " mount upon my horse, and I will go on foot."

The old man would not accept the offer ; the emperor then hit upon the expedient of taking him up behind him on his horse ; but the old man still excused himself, upon the plea that his poverty having deprived him of the means of changing his linen and his clothes, there might be some danger of his catching some vermin from him, from which it was impossible for him to keep free.

"Never mind, my friend," answered the emperor, "get up behind me all the same, I shall only have to change my clothes."

The old man then at last mounted, and they soon arrived both of them at the house to which they were going. No sooner was the emperor there, than he asked for the superintendent, who, on his appearance was exceedingly surprised, when the prince uncovered, to make himself known, the embroidered dragon which he wore in front, and which his hunting dress concealed. It appears that, in order that this memorable act of retributive justice should be rendered more celebrated, the greater number of the grandees who accompanied the emperor out hunting, found themselves assembled round him, as if they had agreed to rendezvous there. For it was in the presence of this large assembly that he showered the bitterest reproaches on the head of the old man's persecutor, and after having compelled him to restore to him his property and his son, he had his head cut off upon the spot. That was not all; he established the old man in his place, and warned him to be careful, seeing a reverse of fortune often changed the disposition, lest others should profit by an injustice on his part as he had just now profited by the injustice of others.

It was on the same principle of justice that the prince, as soon as he attained his majority, punished those of his ministers who had abused his authority while he was a minor. The chief of the four regents, named Sucama, a great persecutor of the Christians, was the first who experienced this justice; for, after being despoiled of his riches, he was condemned to lose his head. It was to a prince so just that God had reserved, as to a second Cyrus, the glory of re-establishing his worship and his altars in China. This was the circumstance which led to it. It is a custom of the Chinese to publish every year the calendar, pretty much as we publish our almanac; but this calendar is considered in that country as a matter of great importance in the state; it is under the control of the public authorities, and even the prince does not disdain to have a hand in it. Since this office had been taken away from father Adam, together with that of president of mathematics, the person who had been appointed in his place had allowed so many mistakes to creep in, that the emperor could bear it no longer, and ordered that it should be revised.

As the courtiers were no longer afraid of giving the prince good advice, to which he always appeared very amenable, there were some honest persons to be found who represented to him that the mathematicians from Europe, who had been exiled during his minority, and three of whom had remained at Pekin, possessed a skill which was well-known throughout all China; that he could not do more wisely than consult them upon the subject. The emperor thought this advice excellent, and forthwith sent for the fathers Ferdinand Verbiest, Louis Buglio, and Gabriel de Magalhans, who were the three who had been retained, and who were far from expecting such agreeable news. The emperor having received them very affably, gave to father Verbiest the calendar to examine which the enemy of the Christians, Yamquam-sien, had drawn up for the ensuing year. The father having taken it and carried it home with him, found more than twenty gross errors, and some of them were so glaring that everybody was surprised at them. He made his report to the emperor, and that prince was so well pleased with it, that he struck up a friendship with this great missionary from that moment, which has been always increasing, and which has now risen to a high point of favour and familiarity. The first use that this new Esdras thought right to make of his influence, was to re-establish the worship of the true God, and to restore to the people the liberty of offering Him the public worship which is His due.

As he was meditating upon the means of accomplishing this object, he found a favourable opportunity in an edict which

the emperor published, ordering that all who had suffered
any oppression during his minority should address themselves to him, and they should obtain justice. Upon this
father Ferdinand resolved to represent to him, that the
greatest injustice which had been done during that time,
was the expulsion from China of the law of the true God,
and the prohibition to the Chinese to observe it. The emperor heard this request with his usual good nature, but not
wishing to dispense with the forms, he sent it to be examined
by a tribunal, which rejected it. The servant of God was
not discouraged. He prayed the emperor to appoint other
judges less prejudiced against the good cause, the present
ones being, as it was well known, much averse to it. The
emperor, with a gracious condescension which was the admiration of all the court, sent the affair to the states of the
empire, who having examined it with the minutest attention,
decided that the Christian religion had been unjustly condemned; that it was good, and that it contained nothing
contrary to the well-being of the kingdom; consequently, that
the memory of father Adam, which had been dishonoured
on account of his having preached it, should be cleared; the
grandees who had been deprived of their offices for having
followed it should be restored, the European priests should
be recalled, Yan-kan-cien condemned to death, and his wife
sent into banishment.

This decision carried great weight, and secured the prince _{Re-esta-}
from the importunate remonstrances of the enemies of reli- in China.
gion. For, although, in order to preserve an appearance of
moderation, he hesitated some time longer, he could not hold
out against the prayers of father Ferdinand, and recalled the
preachers of the gospel from their exile, permitted them to
return to their churches, and to perform their functions, and
condemned their persecutor to banishment, where he died.
He added a prohibition against any one becoming a Christian
in future; but the event has proved that he only inserted that

clause to satisfy some powerful mandarins, who were inimical
to Christianity.   For in the course of the first year that the
preachers returned to their churches, which was the year
1671, at the beginning of September, more than twenty
thousand souls embraced the faith without meeting with any
molestation.   The following year a maternal uncle of the
emperor, and one of the eight perpetual generals who command the Tartar militia, received baptism, and from that
time the gospel has spread so widely over China, that the
number of Christians is estimated at three hundred thousand.

Providence, which never will be outdone in liberality,
has amply recompensed this monarch for what he has done
towards the restoration of the true religion in his dominions,
by sustaining his throne, which was shaken by the revolt of
his subjects, and by enabling him to extend the conquests of
his fathers through the very channel which had almost caused
their loss.   It was in the year 1672 that this rebellion was
begun by Usanguey.   This chieftain had lived peacefully up
to this time in the enjoyment of a fortune, which, while it
kept him aloof from public affairs, still left him enough consideration and wealth to satisfy a moderate man.   The emperor had honoured him with the title of king in the province
of Younan, one of the richest in China.   He did not govern
it because he was king.   For those sorts of kings only have
the title, the paraphernalia, and the honours, but they do
not interfere with the government, the mandarins whom the
emperor sends having all the authority.   The emperors of
the Taimingien family, whose policy could not suffer any of
their relations to take any part in the administration of the
state, or to live at court, had honoured their blood with these
specious titles, which, from the numbers that there were of
these princes in the empire, had become too common to be
of any importance.

The Tartar emperors, who had only given them to a few

persons, and those persons deserving of them, had raised their value greatly, and those whom they had gratified had acted so skilfully, that, without possessing a character for the administration of the affairs of their provinces, they had made themselves masters of them. Usanguey acquired a credit and a reputation in his own, which made him an object of dread at court, whither he never went, and upon which the ministers thought him not dependent enough. They had dissembled their uneasiness with regard to him, as long as they had thought it safe to do so. The affairs of the emperor were now in a state which made it possible to act without danger. All China had submitted to the new dominion; the race of the Taimingien princes was extinct; the Chinese, who were beginning to taste the blessings of peace, did not seem to possess a sufficiently martial spirit to induce them to renew the war. The court even held hostages for the fidelity of Usanguey; for he had not been able to refuse to send his only son there, who had taken with him two of his children.

The ministers, possessed of these pledges, and thinking it advisable to suffer no longer the exorbitant power of Usanguey, meditated his destruction, and in order to attain this object more certainly they invited him, under pretext of doing him honour, to come and enjoy nearer at hand the favours of the government and the attentions of the young monarch. Usanguey, whether it was that he was warned, or that he suspected the trap which lay in wait for him, excused himself from making the journey; but being well aware that an excuse would be ill-received by persons who were accustomed to exact obedience, he was careful to take precautions against their resentment. He sent word to his friends, and was so well supported by them, that in a short time he had troops enough to place him out of danger of being insulted. Some say, that in order to raise the credit of his party amongst the Chinese, he spread abroad the rumour that he had brought up secretly in his palace a son

of the last emperor of China. However this may be, Usanguey, finding himself in a condition to defy the Tartars,
raised the standard of rebellion. It is not to be supposed
that he took this step without a severe conflict with his feelings of paternal affection, which placed before his eyes the
inevitable destruction of the three children which he had at
court ; but he considered himself driven to make this terrible
sacrifice for the sake of his own preservation and the liberty
of his country, the last serving as a decent pretext for saving
his own life in preference to those of his children. In
order to give greater prominence to this motive for his rebellion, he put forth a manifesto, which I subjoin, exactly as I
find it in the manuscript narrative of father Greslon, from
which I have taken this.

" When I summoned the Tartars," he said, " to the assistance of the emperor my master, against the rebels who
attacked him, and who endeavoured to usurp the monarchy,
I gave an opportunity without intending it to these nations
to seize upon it themselves. It now causes me the most
painful regret, and my conscience reproaches me continually
for the evil I have brought down upon my country, by reducing it beneath this tyrannical yoke. I am afraid that
heaven will be irritated against me, and will punish me
severely, if I do not make every effort to repair my fault.
I have been for a long time reflecting upon the means, and
making the necessary preparations for the execution of this
enterprise. If my fellow-countrymen will assist me in the
smallest degree to carry out my design, we shall accomplish it with ease. I have four hundred thousand men devoted to me, without reckoning the auxiliary troops which
are promised me from various kingdoms ; and I am in no
want of money to maintain them. I therefore invite all
brave Chinese to join themselves to me, to drive from the
heart of our country that common enemy which oppresses
her."

This manifesto was the signal for war. The Tartars saw the first outburst without emotion, thinking their dominion too firmly established for them to fear a popular rising ; but they found out afterwards, that amongst newly-conquered subjects, a prince is never secure from revolts. This one found at once the grandees of China so favourably disposed towards it, that in an instant the whole empire was in a flame. The kings of Fokien and of Canton set the example to the rest. He of Fokien, named Kenvan, was displeased with the emperor, who transferred him to Leauton, although he had paid (into the exchequer) one thousand six hundred millions of livres that he might be retained in his post. He of Canton was engaged in the party, in spite of himself, by his son, named Gantacum.

The arms of the allied princes were at first so successful, that the court of Pekin was filled with consternation. Not only the provinces where they dwelt surrendered to them without resistance, but each pushing his conquests into those which were his neighbours, the emperor found himself so closely pressed, that no one doubted that he would abandon Pekin and retire into Tartary. Father Ferdinand assures us that he had already begun to prepare for the journey, never doubting that the emperor would take him with him.

Usanguey, who made use of everything, held secret communications with the court, by means of which he could have cut off the retreat to Tartary had they not been detected. For he had in Pekin itself more than fifty thousand men in his pay, who had been gained over to his party by his emissaries. In four days they were to burn the palace, and cut down every person they should find in it, when one of the conspirators, having too earnestly pressed an armourer, of whom he had ordered some arms, to let him have them by a certain day, this artisan was led to suspect something, and gave information to the magistrates. The Tartars had too good cause to distrust the Chinese at that time to neglect

8

such a warning. They arrested the man named by the
armourer, put him to the question, and drew from him a
confession of the whole. They learnt thereby the names
of the head and the principal members of the conspiracy.
Those who had not had time to fly were punished, and being
unable to revenge themselves on Usanguey in person, they
punished him in the person of his children, whom their kindness up to that time had spared notwithstanding the rebellion
of their father. He even chose for them the mode of death
which amongst those nations is considered the most honourable, by sending them a piece of white silk to serve as a cord
by which they might strangle themselves, thus permitting
them to put an end to their lives with their own hands. It
does not appear that this honour afforded much consolation
to the three unhappy princes in their misfortune. They
testified extreme regret in quitting life, which up to that time
they had found highly agreeable. For as they were handsome and well born, they were tenderly loved by all re-
spectable persons at the court, even by the emperor, who
apparently only proceeded to this extremity against them in
order to deprive the rebel, their father, of the advantage he
might have drawn from them to add credit to his party.
The youngest, who was only ten years old, strengthened the
courage of his father and his brother, who shrunk from the
sight of the preparations for their death, and who could not
muster up resolution to inflict it upon themselves.

" As there is no more hope," he said to them, " let us do
speedily and with a good grace what necessity has imposed
upon us."

And having said these words, he placed his neck in the
noose which had been prepared ; and the two others having
followed his example, all three thus terminated their lives.

Usanguey felt his loss to a degree which was far beyond
what one might imagine, and the desire of avenging his relatives, added to the love of liberty, animated him with a

hatred of the Tartars, which made him swear to put to death all who by the chances of war should fall into his hands. And to show to all his party that he never meant to be reconciled to them, and not choosing to take the name of emperor himself, because, he said, he was too old to change his condition, he caused it to be assumed by his grandson, the only one who remained to him.

The Tartar emperor, on his side, not losing courage amidst the general consternation which the earlier successes of Usanguey had spread amongst his people, showed by his conduct on this occasion, that the ingenuity and the constancy of a wise philosopher ride through the greatest storms. His resolution imparted itself to others, and the fortunate discovery of the conspiracy having proved to him that his good fortune had not deserted him, the courage of the Tartars revived, and they resumed their former energy. This new ardour having spread from the court to the troops, who were divided into different bodies, according as they were required in the different places where the rebels had carried the war, the torrent of conquest already achieved by Usanguey was arrested, and a battle was gained against the king of Fokien, in which he suffered great loss. This prince had already nearly joined to the province which he inhabited that of Kiamsi, which is close by. He had made himself master of three large towns, and having an army of one hundred and fifty thousand men, he doubted not that the remainder would soon yield to his power ; when, about five or six miles above Kienchamp, which he had just reduced to submission, he encountered a Tartar army commanded by Sumvan, uncle to the emperor, who opposed his progress. The Chinese prince considered this army, which was far inferior to his own in numbers, and which he imagined was composed of surprised troops, as an insignificant obstacle to his conquest ; but the event proved to him that he was mistaken. For the Tartar prince having offered him battle, defeated him in the open field, and made such a carnage of his army, which was entirely composed of raw troops, too ignorant in military tactics to make use of the resources of war, that the whole field of battle and the neighbouring country was encumbered with the corpses of the slain. The number was so great, that as no one would take the trouble to afford them sepulture, the air was so much infected that a pestilence followed closely upon the war, and completed the desolation of the country. A river which was near the place where they had fought became so choked with dead bodies, that the waters remained long tainted.

Upon the rumour of this defeat, the garrison, which the Chinese general had left at Kiencham, was seized with a panic, and left the city. The inhabitants followed, and each escaped as he best could. The victor, who, after the battle, had advanced against this town with the intention of laying siege to it, and never doubting that he would meet with a severe resistance, was very much astonished when he found all the gates open. At first he feared some stratagem, but the skirmishers of his army having advanced, and having ascertained that there was no one in the houses, the general gave the word to enter, and gave up the place to pillage. The Tartar soldier did not content himself with the booty he found in the town; he proceeded to search in the neighbourhood for the inhabitants, who were concealed in different places, and practised a thousand cruelties upon them. The general was blamed at court for having permitted this violence, and, however great were the obligations which the emperor felt he owed him, his sense of justice would not permit him to leave this action unpunished, for he disgraced him for some time, and deprived him of all his pensions when the war was terminated; prudence and the need in which he stood of his services not allowing him to do this sooner.

Father Greslon said that he came to Nancham at the time of this devastation, the Tartar army being still there, and he asserts that this town lost during all this war as many as one hundred and six thousand inhabitants, exclusive of seventy-five thousand whom the Tartars carried away captive. The Jesuits had a beautiful church there and a flourishing religion, which this tempest destroyed. The general was nevertheless fond of the Christians, and of the fathers in particular. Putting aside the action of which we have been speaking, and to which he was incited by the ardour of war, he is a great man, full of good qualities, and to whom the Christian religion owes its restoration in China, as the Tartars owe to him in a great degree the preservation of their conquest. Moreover he showed on this occasion a thousand marks of kindness to father Greslon, who went to pay him a visit. For he came two or three times to his church, turned out an officer and forty soldiers who had taken possession of it, and gave the father letters of protection, not only for that church, but for all those in the province. So that one may say that he did more for the preservation of the Christian churches than of the temples of his idols.

The Tartar general having thought it necessary to remain some time in his conquests in order to establish the emperor's authority, sent during this time to Fokien, where Kenvan had retired, to offer him an amnesty on the part of the prince if he would return to his allegiance. As there was a friendship between them, Sumvan did all he could to get him out of his predicament and thereby shorten the war, but he could not accomplish it. While he was negotiating with Kenvan to induce him to submit to the emperor, Kenvan was negotiating with Chin, that son of Quesin, who, as we have said, made himself king of Formosa in order to sustain the rebellion. Chin, who was only too happy to have such an opportunity of entering China, did not require much pressing. He presented himself to Kenvan and brought him some troops, who would have been more useful to the common cause of the confederates if they had not been so

powerful. For Chin, finding himself far superior to Kenvan
in the numbers and quality of his soldiers, from being his
ally wished to become his master. He refused to treat him
as a king. It is even said, that in order to avenge the
death of his grandfather Icoan, in which it was reported that
the father of Kenvan had assisted, he attempted his life.
This alliance, which turned out so unfortunate, induced
Kenvan to think of returning to his allegiance. He made
his terms with the emperor, from whom he asked for troops
to drive out Chin from the province of Fokien. The emperor shewed great ability in making use of one enemy to
destroy the other. He sent his troops to Fokien, which
having, with the aid of Kenvan, forced Chin to re-cross the
sea, took possession of this province ; and taking from the
king the command which he held in the army, they only left
him four hundred men for the security of his person, with
whom they banished him to a maritime fortress to defend it
against Chin, the emperor deferring till another period his
intention of making a more terrible example of this man,
whose compulsory penitence could not efface the memory of
his too voluntary crime.

The evil fortune of the king of Fokien, made the king of
Canton begin to apprehend lest his own might not be invariably good. Up to this time it had been so, but he had
reason to fear that it might not continue. Usanguey did not
treat him well, he refused him the title of king, and assumed
an air of superiority which displeased him. Besides, he saw
that the party of the League was much enfeebled by the
successes that the Tartars had obtained over Kenvan. All
these considerations made him resolve to negotiate with the
emperor for peace. He even persuaded Gantacum, his son,
to condescend to the same step, who, although he did not
like the Tartars, and never had liked them, as he has since
declared to some persons to whom he was speaking confi-
dentially, nevertheless was compelled by the necessity of his

affairs to serve them very usefully. For the king his father
having made peace with the emperor, he wrote to Pekin for
troops, in order to reduce some towns in his province which
still held out for Usanguey. They sent him some, and he
made such good use of them, that not only he took those
towns, but, having even given battle to a considerable body
of the rebel troops, he defeated them. The court approved
so highly of this action, that, his father dying at this juncture, the emperor confirmed him in his dignity and posses-
sions.

The new king seemed grateful for these favours. For,
not satisfied with having replaced the province of Canton
under the Tartar dominion, he did the same by a portion of
that of Quamsi, which he took from Usanguey. He was
about to reduce the remainder, but domestic treachery arrested the course of his victories ; and he whom the brave
Usanguey had been unable to overcome, perished by the
perfidy of two or three wretches. The viceroy of the province, an officer of his army, and the intendant of his household, were the authors of this infamous deed. These villains,
who evidently intended to divide his property, having con-
spired his downfall by one of the blackest crimes recorded
in history, employed the name of his mother and his own
money to accomplish it. For it was in the name of his
mother that they wrote to the emperor a malignant and
artful letter, in which she gave information of a new scheme
of rebellion plotted against the state by her son ; and it was
with the money of this prince that the intendant corrupted
those who were about the person of the emperor, in order to
hasten his master's ruin.

The intrigue succeeded as well as they could desire.
Their letter and their partisans blinded the justice of the
emperor, whose fears being easily roused at a juncture in
which Usanguey was still in arms, gave orders to some
Tartar officers instantly to seize upon the person of the un-

happy king of Canton. When the officers had arrived upon
the spot, they found that their orders were not so easy of
execution as it had been supposed at the court. This king
was at the head of a victorious army, who adored him. In
consequence, it was more than six months before they could
undertake anything against him, and if they had not made
use of a stratagem, they would not have accomplished it.
They caught him by his weak point. He was fond of drinking. They invited him to an entertainment, to which having
repaired with only a few followers, he was seized and conducted to Canton in such haste, that his soldiers hearing of
the arrest of their general too late, despaired of being able to
follow him.

They reserved themselves in order to be able to serve him
more usefully afterwards, but unfortunately for them the
emperor's party was the strongest in Canton. All those who
had been able had introduced themselves quietly into the
town, and waited, in order to declare themselves, to see the
issue of the affair, which seemed likely to linger on for some
time ; not wishing, by any premature demonstration, to turn
a doubtful cause into a bad one. While they were in this
suspense, a rumour spread through the town that the king
was condemned to death. This news obliged his friends to
throw off the mask and to rush to arms. They ran to the
prison where he was confined, and endeavoured to force the
doors. They were led by the brothers of this prince, who
had vowed to rescue him at the peril of their heads. As
they were all brave and well armed, they attacked the guards
with great fury, and these would have offered no resistance
if the Tartar garrison, which was strong, had not hastened
to their assistance. The combat was sanguinary and obstinate, and there were many killed on both sides ; but the
Tartars conquered at last, and the enterprise of the Chinese
only placed their king in a more culpable light.

As misfortunes never come alone, the mother of this prince,

by a zeal quite as ill-timed as that of his friends, greatly aggravated his crime. The perfidious officer of whom we have spoken, who, in concert with the viceroy, had laboured to effect the ruin of Gantacum, had fallen in love with one of his wives, who had the reputation of being the greatest beauty in China. This passion so completely blinded him, that he had the audacity to pursue her even into the apartment of the queen to carry her off to his house. The lady resisted as long as she could, but, to defend herself against a man who had all the strength on his side, she had no weapons but her cries. Even he was touched, and wishing to console her, he told her that he would make her queen, and that she would not repent of having quitted a master and the condition of a slave, to take a husband whom she would rule as mistress. These promises, far from consoling the lady, roused her anger ; so that, assuming a lofty tone, she said to him with an air of profound disdain : "You will make me queen ! and pray what reason have you for flattering yourself that you will ever be king ? Begone, remain satisfied with what you are, and take care that your ambition, instead of raising a throne for you, does not dig you a precipice."

The haughty mandarin could not endure these words, and his rage was so violent, that passing on the instant from one extreme to the other, he drew his scimiter, and before the very eyes of the queen he slew this woman, who was considered far happier to have incurred his hatred than to have deserved his love. Such an extraordinary act filled all upright people with horror, and the queen mother of the imprisoned king, to whom the emperor, who thought she was in his interest in opposition to that of her son, still left considerable power, resolved to avenge the crime. In order to secure her revenge, she had the cunning to engage the murderer to pay her a visit, under pretext of consulting with him upon an affair which concerned the court. He came, and he found there the punishment due to so many crimes, being despatched with a poniard as he entered the apartment of this princess.

The prisoner, who up to this moment knew nothing of what was passing, learned this news by accident, for the room in which he was confined being rather near his kitchen, he overheard the cooks, who were talking over the affair, and who related so many of the circumstances that he made out the whole history. He had not yet lost hope, but this incident was enough to destroy it.

" I am lost," he cried; " this violence, executed at such an unfortunate moment upon an officer of the emperor's, will be laid to my charge, and 1 shall not be forgiven."

In fact, it is thought that this hastened his death, for a short time after two Tartar mandarins appeared, who had made the journey from Pekin in seventeen days, and who brought to the prisoner the fatal present of the piece of white stuff which the Chinese emperors give to criminals of rank whom they condemn to death. Some persons relate that two executioners strangled him, and that he refused the impious honour of dying by his own hand, alleging as an excuse, that it was not permitted to men thus to put an end to their own lives. His habits of intercourse with the Christians had inspired him with this sentiment, for he loved the ministers of the gospel, and during their exile in Canton he always had two Jesuits with him. He often said that the love of women was the only thing which prevented him from receiving baptism. He exhorted his servants to receive it, and he said that he thought himself unfortunate not to have obtained the proper dispositions for the reception of this sacrament. He asked one day, if a man who should only receive it at his death, or who was unable to receive it, would not be saved by praying for forgiveness from God? His connexion with the Christians, made them fear after his death that his friendship would prove fatal to them ; for, upon leaving the

prison where he had been executed, the mandarins demanded to be led to the church. Father Couplet, who was
there at the time, told me that this sudden visit at such a
moment had caused great terror ; but they were soon reassured when the mandarins, after saluting them with civility,
gave them a letter from father Ferdinand, which they accompanied with every possible token of consideration and regard.
The same father accompanied them to Macao, whither they
went on the part of the emperor, to thank that town for a
lion which it had made him a present of, and with which he
had been the more pleased because it had been refused to
Usanguey.

Moreover it was running a considerable risk to affront that
general, whose power was still considerable, and who, notwithstanding the ill-success of his allies, maintained during
the remainder of his life his dignity and his reputation
against all the efforts of the Tartar power. It was fortunate
for them that he was old. For though his party was weakened, and he had even lost some of his conquests, he was
still powerful enough to give a great deal of trouble to the
emperor. His death, which occurred in the year 1679, was
a proof of the good fortune of this prince, which, after being
for a while unfaithful to him, always returned to him. The
war lasted two years after the death of the great Usanguey,
his party having refused the amnesty which the emperor had
offered to them. This general had entrusted the guardian-
ship of his successor, who was still too young to support the
weight of affairs which devolved upon him, to a captain, one
of his friends, to whom, when he was dying, he had given
the command of his troops ; but he had neither given him
his ability nor his good fortune. For the Tartar army, after
hotly pursuing him for some time, defeated him in the year
1681 in a great battle ; after which, the heir of Usanguey
was reduced to such extremity, that he died by his own
hand, and left the emperor possessor of all that portion

of his conquests which this party had wrested from him.

The emperor victorious over all his enemies. His power and the extent of his empire.

There was left only the island of Formosa, which had not submitted to the yoke. Chin, who was in possession of it, seemed to have become invincible from the number of his ships: at the same time it was important to the emperor that he should be subdued. In order to be more certain of attaining his object, he sent an offer to the Dutch to restore to them what they had possessed in this island, with the title of king for him whom they should name, if they would assist him with their fleet to accomplish its reduction.

Some historians write that Riclof, who was general of Batavia, did not answer the offers of the emperor as that prince would have wished, alleging that he could not undertake any enterprise of the kind without the orders of the company, for which he would have to wait till they arrived from Holland. However this may be, the emperor resolved to attack Chin, and to reduce Formosa under the dominion of the crown of China. I find a discrepancy in the accounts that have been written of the reduction of this great island. It is however agreed upon, and we may safely say, until this point is cleared up, that the emperor is now master of it, and that this prince is thus the peaceful possessor of three great monarchies, China, Niuchè, and Tamgu; by which, if we may add the tributary kingdoms of Corea, of Cochinchina, of Tonquin, and many others, it will be seen that this monarch may boast of having the most extensive and populous empire in the world, as it is one of the finest, the most flourishing, and the best regulated.

The magnificence of the emperor of China.

The magnificence of this prince corresponds with the greatness of the empire. His train, his residences, his armies, everywhere bear this reputation. In the last four or five years he has made journeys in various parts of his dominions, where his mode of travelling and his suite, presented to the view a pomp and regal splendour that is difficult to conceive. The first was in Western Tartary, after he had punished

Kenvan, king of Fokien, one of the rebels, whom he had cajoled up to that moment. I subjoin the account which father Verbiest has given of it, in which, besides the part which concerns the prince, the reader will find some useful and curious remarks giving information upon the country.[1]

The emperor of China made a journey into Oriental Tar- Relation of a journey of tary at the commencement of this year, 1682, after having, by the emperor into Eastern the death of three rebel kings, suppressed a revolt which Tartary. had been formed in some of the provinces of the empire. One of these rebel princes was strangled in the province of which he had made himself master. The second, having been conducted to Pekin, with the principal chiefs of his faction, was cut to pieces in sight of the whole court, the most considerable among the mandarins assisting with their own hands at this melancholy execution, to revenge upon this rebel the fate of their relatives, who had been cruelly put to death by him. The third, who was the most important, and, as it were, the head of the whole rebellion, had anticipated by voluntary death the punishment he deserved, and thus put an end to a war which had lasted seven years.

Peace having been thus re-established in the empire, and all the provinces enjoying their ancient liberty in quiet, the emperor set out on the 23rd of March to go to the province of Leauton, which is the country of his ancestors, for the purpose of visiting their sepulchres, and after having honoured them with the usual ceremonies, to follow the road to Eastern Tartary. This journey was about one thousand one hundred miles, from Pekin to the other extremity.

The emperor took with him his eldest son, a young prince

---

[1] The text of this and another letter by father Verbiest, describing his two journeys in the suite of the Emperor into Tartary, is considerably modified by the Père d'Orleans from the Dutch, as we find it given by Witzen in his " Noord en Oost Tartarien," tom. i, p. 185. For this reason a translation from the Dutch is inserted at the end of this volume, in the form of an appendix.

*

ten years of age, who is already declared heir to the empire. The three principal queens also went this journey, each one in a gilded chariot; the principal kings who compose this empire were there also, with all the grandees of the court, and the most considerable mandarins of all the orders, who having all a very large retinue, and a numerous attendance, formed a cortège for the emperor of more than seventy thousand persons.

He desired that I also should accompany him in this journey, and that I should always be near him, that I might make in his presence the observations necessary to know the disposition of the heavens, the elevation of the pole, and the declination of each country, and to measure by mathematical instruments the height of mountains and the distances of places. He was also very glad to gain information respecting meteors, and on many other physical and mathematical subjects. For this purpose an officer was charged to convey upon horses the instruments of which I had need, and he commended me to the care of the prince his uncle, who is also his father-in-law, and the second person in the state : he is called by a Chinese title, signifying Associate of the empire. He charged him to provide all things necessary for me during the journey, of which charge this prince acquitted himself with great kindness, causing me always to lodge in his own tent and to eat at his table.

The emperor ordered that I should have horses supplied me from his own stable, and a sufficient number of them for me to change them at my convenience; and among those which were given me, were some that he had mounted himself, which is a very great distinction. In this journey our march was constantly towards the summer east.

From Pekin to the province of Leauton the road, which is about thirty miles, is tolerably level. Even in the province of Leauton it is forty miles, but much more unequal, because of the mountains. From the frontier of this province to the town of Ula, by which passes the river, called by the Tartars Songoro, and by the Chinese Sum-hoa, the road, which is yet four hundred miles in length, is very difficult of passage, being interrupted sometimes by extremely steep mountains, sometimes by valleys of extraordinary depth, and by desert plains, where for two or three days' journey nothing is to be seen. The mountains of this country are covered on the eastern side by large oaks and ancient forests, which have not been cut for centuries.

All the country which is beyond the province of Leauton is very barren; nothing is to be seen on all sides but mountains, valleys, caves of tigers, bears, and other wild beasts: scarcely any houses are to be found, but only wretched cottages upon the banks of rivers and torrents. All the towns and villages which I have seen in Leauton, and of which there was a pretty large number, were entirely in ruins. Everywhere there were old ruined houses, with fragments of stone and brick. In the enclosure of these towns are some houses newly built, but without order: some are made of earth, others of the remains of the old buildings, the most part covered with straw, very few with brick. At present there remains not the slightest vestige of a great number of towns and villages which existed before the war; for the petty kings of the Tartars who commenced it, having at first but a very small army, made the inhabitants of those places take to arms, and destroyed them afterwards, that the soldiers might have no hope of ever returning to their country.

The capital of Leauton, which is called Xin-yam, is a tolerably handsome and complete city; it has even yet the remains of an ancient palace. As far as I have been able to judge by frequent observations, it is in forty-one degrees fifty-six minutes; that is to say, two degrees above Pekin, though, up to the present time, both Europeans and Chinese have only given it forty-one degrees. There is not in this city any declination of the needle, as I have remarked by many repeated

observations.   The city of Ula, which was nearly the termination of our journey, is in forty-one degrees twenty minutes.
The declination of the compass at this place is one degree
forty minutes from south to west.

But to resume the course of our journey.   From Pekin, as
far as this eastern extremity, a new road was made, by which
the emperor could travel conveniently on horseback, and the
queens in their chariots.   This road is about ten feet wide,
as straight and as level as it was possible to make it.   It
extends nearly one thousand one hundred miles.   On each
side is made a kind of little bank, a foot high, always equal
and perfectly parallel the one to the other : and this road
was also as clean, especially in fine weather, as the floor
where the labourers thresh the corn in the fields ; there were
also people upon the road, who had nothing to do but to
keep it clean.   Christians do not take so much care to sweep
the streets and public places by which the holy Sacrament
passes in processions, as these infidels do to clean the roads
by which their kings and queens are to pass every time they
leave their palace.

A road was made for the return similar to the first.   The
mountains had been levelled as much as possible, the bridges
over the torrents had been repaired, and for ornament a kind of
mat had been extended on each side, upon which were painted
divers figures of animals, which produced the same effect as
the tapestries which are hung out in the streets at processions.

The emperor scarcely ever followed this road, as he was
hunting almost constantly.   And even when he joined the
queens, he rode by their side alone, for fear the great number
of horses in his suite should incommode them.   He rode generally at the head of this kind of army.   The queens immediately
followed in their chariots, with their retinue and baggage.
Some interval was left, nevertheless, between him and them.
Then came the kings, the grandees of the court, and the

mandarins, each according to his rank. An infinite number of servants and others on horseback formed the rear guard.

As there was no city in all the route which could furnish lodging for so great a number of people, or provide them with food; and as, besides, great part of the journey was through places little inhabited, we were obliged to carry with us all that was necessary for the journey, and even provisions for three months.

For this reason an infinite number of waggons, camels, horses, and mules to carry the baggage were sent before, by roads which had been made by the side of the emperor's. Besides this the emperor, the kings, and almost all the grandees of the court, had a great number of led horses to follow, that they might change from time to time. I do not reckon the droves of oxen, and sheep, and other cattle which they were obliged to bring. And though this great multitude of men, horses, and flocks, went by a road at some distance from that of the emperor, they raised, nevertheless, such a horrible dust, that we seemed to go in a cloud, and could scarcely distinguish at fifteen or twenty paces those who went before us.

The road was so well marked out, that the army encamped every evening on the banks of some river or torrent. Early in the morning the tents and necessary baggage were sent forward, and the marshals of the stations arriving first, marked out the place most proper for the tent of the emperor, for those of the queens, the kings, the grandees of the court, and the mandarins, according to the dignity of each, and his rank in the Chinese army, which is divided into eight orders or eight standards.

In the space of three months we advanced more than nine hundred miles towards the north-east. At length we arrived at Kam-Hay, which is a fort situated between the South Sea and the Mountains of the North. It is here that the celebrated wall commences, which separates the province

of Leauton from that of Pekin, called Pequeli, and it extends
to an immense distance northwards, passing over the highest
mountains. When we had entered into this province, the
emperor, the kings, and the grandees of the court, left the
great road of which we have spoken, and took that of the
Mountains of the North, which extends without interrup-
tion towards the north-east. They passed here several days
in the chase, which was managed in this manner.

The emperor chose three thousand men of his body
guards, armed with arrows and javelins, and dispersed
them on all sides, so that they made a great circuit round
the mountains, which they surrounded entirely. In this
way they made a kind of circle, of which the diameter was at
least three thousand paces. Then approaching each other with
even steps, without quitting their ranks, whatever obstacles
they might find in their road (for the emperor had interspersed
among them, officers, and even grandees of the court, to
maintain order), they reduced the large circle to one much
smaller, which was about three hundred paces in diameter ;
thus all the animals which had been enclosed in the first,
found themselves taken as it were in a net, because each
man planting his foot on the earth, they closed in against each
other so compactly, that there was no chance of escape.
Then they pursued them so quickly in this little space, that
the poor animals, too exhausted to run, fell at the feet of the
hunters, and suffered themselves to be easily taken. I have
seen two or three hundred hares, at least, tàken in this manner in one day, without reckoning an infinite number of
wolves and foxes. I have seen the same thing many times
in Tartary, beyond the province of Leauton, where I remember to have seen among others more than one thousand stags
shut up in this kind of net, which, finding no way of saving
themselves, threw themselves into the hands of the hunters.
They kill'd also bears, wild boars, and more than sixty tigers.
But these they take in another manner, and make use of
other arms.

The emperor wished that I should go to all the different hunts, and in a very kind manner recommended me to the particular care of his father-in-law, who was not to suffer me to be exposed to any danger during the hunting of tigers or any other ferocious beasts. I was the only one among the mandarins without arms, and near to the emperor. Although I had had little to fatigue me since we began our journey, I found myself so weary every evening on arriving at my tent, that I could not support myself, and I would many times have avoided following the emperor, if my friends had not advised me to the contrary, and if I had not feared he might have taken it ill if he had perceived it.

After having gone about four hundred miles, always hunting in this manner, we arrived at length at Xinyam, the chief city of the province, where we stayed four days. The inhabitants of Corea came and presented to the emperor a sea-calf which they had taken. The emperor showed it to me, and asked me if in any of our European books this fish was mentioned. I told him we had a book in our library at Pekin, which explained its nature, and in which there was a picture of it; he showed great desire to see it, and very soon dispatched a courier to the fathers at Pekin, who brought it to me in a few days. The emperor was pleased to find that the description of the fish in the book agreed with what he had seen. He caused it then to be taken to Pekin, to be there carefully preserved among the curiosities of the Palace.

During the stay which we made in this city, the emperor went with the queens to visit the tombs of his ancestors, which were not far distant; from hence he sent back the princesses to Xinyam, and continued his journey towards Eastern Tartary.

After many days of marching and hunting he arrived at Kirin, which is four hundred miles distant from Xinyam. This city is built along the great river Songoro, which rises in Mont Champé, distant from hence four hundred miles towards the south. This mountain, so famous in the east for having been the ancient dwelling of the Tartars, is always covered with snow, from which it takes its name; for Champé signifieth " white mountain."

As soon as the emperor perceived it, he descended from his horse, kneeled on the bank, and bowed three times to the earth to salute it. Then he caused himself to be carried on a throne, brilliant with gold, and thus made his entrance into the city. The people ran in crowds before him, and expressed by their tears the joy they felt in seeing him. The prince took great pleasure in these testimonies of affection, and to show his good will to them, he wished that every one might see him, and would not allow his guards to prevent the people from approaching him, as they did in Pekin.

In this city they make their boats in a particular manner. The inhabitants always keep a great number in readiness to repulse the Muscovites, who often come upon this river to contend with them in the pearl fisheries. The emperor rested here two days, after which he descended the river with several lords, accompanied by more than one hundred boats, as far as the city of Ula, which is the most beautiful in all the country, and which was formerly the seat of Tartar empire.

A little below this city, which is at most thirty-two miles from Kirin, the river is full of a certain fish, which much resembles the plaice[1] of Europe; and it was principally for the amusement of catching these fish, that the emperor went to Ula: but the rains coming suddenly, swelled the river so much, that all the nets were broken and carried away by the force of the water. The emperor meanwhile remained five or six days at Ula; but seeing that the rains did not cease, he was obliged to return to Kirin, without having had

[1] The fish here called plaice, is described in the Dutch as " steur," a sturgeon. See the translation from the Dutch in the Appendix.

the pleasure of fishing. As we reascended the river, the vessel in which I was with the father-in-law of the emperor, was so damaged by the violence of the waves, that we were compelled to land, and to mount a chariot drawn by an ox, which brought us very late to Kirin, the rain continuing the whole of the way.

That evening, as we talked over the adventure with the emperor, he said merrily: " The fish has made sport of us." At last, after remaining two days at Kirin, the rains began to abate, and we resumed our journey to Leauton. I cannot express here the pains and fatigue which we endured during all the course of this journey, by roads which the waters had spoiled, and rendered almost impassable. Our way was constantly by mountains or by valleys, and it was not without extreme danger that we could pass the torrents and rivers, which were swelled from the ravines, whose waters fall into them on all sides. The bridges were either thrown down by the violence of the currents, or covered by the overflowing of the waters. There were in many places great collections of water and mud, from which it was almost impossible to extricate one's self. The horses, camels, and other beasts of burden, which carried the baggage, could not go on ; they sunk in the mud of the morasses, or died of fatigue on the roads. The men were not less distressed, and all were weakened by want of food and the refreshments necessary for so long a journey. Numbers of horsemen were obliged to go on foot leading their horses, which could do no more, or to stop in the middle of the road to let them recover their breath. Though the marshalls of the stations spared neither labour nor wood, which they cut on all sides, in order to fill up all these bad roads with faggots : yet after the horses and chariots, which since early morning had taken the lead, were once passed, it was impossible to pass after them ; the emperor even, with the prince his son, and all the great lords of the court, were obliged more than once to go on foot over the mud and the

morasses, fearing to expose themselves to a greater danger
if they attempted to pass on horseback.

When they came to bridges or defiles all the army stopped,
and when the emperor had passed, with those of the highest
consequence, all the rest of the multitude came in crowds,
and as each wished to pass first, many were thrown into the
water : others taking byways still more dangerous, fell into
bogs and mire, from which they could not extricate themselves.   In fact, there was so much to suffer in all the roads
of Eastern Tartary, that old officers, who had followed the
court for more than thirty years, said they had never suffered so much as on this journey.

It was on these occasions that the emperor more than once
showed proofs of remarkable kindness towards me, and took
such care of me that I was at a loss to know how to acknowledge it.

The first day that we took the road for our return, we
were stopped in the evening by a torrent so large and rapid
that it was impossible to ford it.

The emperor having found there by chance a little vessel
which would carry four persons at most, crossed first with
the prince.   Some of the kings then passed over.   All
the others, princes, lords, and mandarins with the rest of
the army, meanwhile, impatiently waited on the bank the
return of the vessel, that they might at least gain the other side
of the torrent, because night was coming on, and the tents had
been carried over long before.   But the emperor returning to
us in a little vessel like the first, called aloud to know where
I was, and the prince, his father-in-law, having presented
me to him, " Let him come," said the emperor, " and pass
over with us."   Thus we went over alone with the emperor,
and all the rest remained on the bank, where they were
obliged to pass the night without shelter.   The same thing
happened the next day nearly in the same manner.   The
emperor found himself at mid-day on the bank of a torrent

as swollen and as rapid as the first. He gave orders that they should make use of the vessels till evening to carry over the tents, the bales, and the rest of the baggage, and afterwards ordered that I should pass over alone with him, and a few of his people, having left on the bank all his great lords, who were obliged to remain there during the night. The father-in-law of the emperor even, having asked if he should not pass over with me, as I lodged in his tent, and ate at his table, was told by the prince to remain, and that he would himself give me all that was necessary.

When we had crossed over, the emperor seated himself on the bank of the water, and made me sit by his side, with the sons of two petty Western kings, and the first Colao of Tartary, whom he treated with distinction on all occasions.

As the night was fine, and the heavens very clear, he wished me to name to him, in the Chinese and European languages, all the constellations which then appeared above the horizon, and he himself first named all those which he knew already. Then unfolding a little map of the heavens, with which I had presented him some years before, he set himself to find the hour of the night by the southern star, pleasing himself by showing to every one the knowledge he had in these sciences. All these marks of kindness, and others of the same kind which he often showed me, even to sending for me to eat at his table,—all these marks, I say, were so public and extraordinary, that the emperor's two uncles, who bore the title of Associates of the empire, said, after they returned to Pekin, that when the emperor had any grief, or was out of spirits, he recovered his wonted cheerfulness when he saw me.

I arrived in perfect health at Pekin, very late on the 9th of June, though some remained ill on the road, or had returned wounded and crippled.

I say nothing of what we did for religion during this journey. The details are reserved for a special narrative, where it will be seen that by the grace of our Lord, our favour at the court of China produced considerable advantage to the Church, yet removed not the cross from the shoulders of the missionaries.

The good effect which this journey had in reviving towards the emperor the affections of his natural subjects, induced him to make one the following year, for the purpose of maintaining in obedience other subjects which he had newly gained in Western Tartary. This has been related by the same father Verbiest in a letter which he wrote on his return.

Account of a second voyage of the emperor in Western Tartary.

In the year 1683, which is the thirtieth of the emperor's age, he made a journey into Western Tartary, with the queen, his grandmother, who is called the queen-mother. He set out on the 6th of July, and wished that I should follow him with one of the two fathers, who were with me at the court; leaving me the choice. I took the father Grimaldi, because he was the best known, and was perfectly well acquainted with mathematics.

Several reasons induced the emperor to undertake this journey. The first was to keep his soldiers in continual exercise during peace, as well as during war; and it is for this reason, that after having established a solid peace in all parts of his vast empire, he has summoned the best troops from each province to be about his person, and has made a resolution in council to effect every year some movements of this nature, in order thus to teach them, while pursuing the chace of wild boars, bears, and tigers, how to conquer the enemies of the empire; or at least to prevent the luxury of China, and too long repose, from weakening their courage and causing their former valour to degenerate.

In fact, this kind of hunting is more like a military expedition, than a party of pleasure. The emperor brings in his suite a hundred thousand horses, and more than sixty thousand men, all armed with arrows and scimitars, divided

by companies and marching in order of battle after their
ensigns, to the sound of drums and trumpets. During the
chase, they invest entire mountains and forests, as if they
were towns which they were besieging, following in this the
manner of hunting of the Eastern Tartars, of which I spoke
in my last letter. This army has its van, its rear-guard,
and the main body; its right wing and its left wing commanded by as many chiefs, who are generally those bearing
the title of king. During the seventy days that they are
marching, the ammunition of the army has to be carried upon
carriages, and horses, through roads which are extremely
difficult to travel over, as Western Tartary is full of mountains and rocks. There are neither cities, towns, nor villages,—there are not even houses. The inhabitants dwell in
tents set up on all sides in the fields. They are for the most
part herdsmen, and transport their tents from one valley to
another, according as the pasture is better for their oxen,
horses, and camels. They have no animals to keep that
require tending, but only those for which the uncultivated
ground will produce herbs of itself. They pass their lives
in the chase, or in doing nothing, and as they neither sow nor
cultivate the ground, they have no harvest. They live on
milk, cheese, and flesh, and they have a kind of wine something resembling our brandy, of which they are very fond,
and with which they are frequently intoxicated. In fact,
they think of nothing but eating and drinking from morning
till night, like the flocks and herds which they keep.

They have priests, whom they call Lamas, and for whom
they have a singular veneration ; in this they differ from the
Eastern Tartars, the greater part of whom have no religion,
and do not believe in God. For the rest, both the one and
the other are slaves, depending entirely on the will of their
masters, following them blindly in religion and habits of life;
thus again resembling their flocks, which go where they are
taken, and not where they would.

11

This part of Tartary is situated beyond the great wall of China, about a thousand Chinese furlongs, that is to say, more than three hundred European miles, and it extends from the summer east[1] towards the north. The emperor goes on horseback at the head of his army by desert places, by steep mountains, and far from the great road, exposed all day to the heat of the sun, to rain, and to all the inclemencies of the weather. Many of those who have been in the late wars, have assured me that they did not endure so much' during that time, as during these huntings ; thus the emperor whose object was to keep the troops in exercise, has effected what he aimed at.

The second reason he had for undertaking this journey, was to keep the Western Tartars to their duty, and prevent the designs they might have formed against the state. It was for this that he entered their country with so large an army, and such grand warlike preparations, taking even artillery, which he caused to be discharged from time to time in the valleys, in order that the noise and fire of the cannons might spread terror all around.

Independent of all this equipage, it was his will that he should be accompanied by all the marks of grandeur which surround him at Pekin. I mean the multitude of drums, trumpets, kettle drums, and other musical instruments, which are played while he is at table, and to the sound of which he enters his palace, and leaves it. He caused all this to accompany him on his march, to astonish these barbarous races with this outward pomp, and to impress on them the fear and the respect which was due to his imperial majesty.

The empire of China has never at any time had enemies more to be feared than these Western Tartars, who beginning from the east of China, surround it with an almost infinite multitude of people, and keep it as if besieged on the

---

[1] The expression thus rendered, is " l'orient d'été," the point where the sun rises at the beginning of summer, when the days are longest.

northern and western sides. And it is to prevent their incursions, that an ancient emperor of China caused the great wall to be built which separates China from their country. I have passed it four times, and have considered it closely. I can say, without exaggeration, that the seven wonders of the world put together are not to be compared to this work; and that all that fame has reported of it in Europe is far below what I have seen of it.

Two things have particularly raised my admiration of it : the first is, that in its long extent from east to west, it passes, in several places, not only by vast plains, but over very high mountains, over which it rises gradually, fortified at intervals by large towers, which are not more distant from each other than two casts of a crossbow. On our return I had the curiosity to measure the height in one place, and I found it to be one thousand and thirty-seven geometric feet above the horizon. It is incomprehensible how they were able to raise this enormous bulwark to the height at which we see it, in dry and mountainous places, where they were obliged to bring from afar, and with incredible labour, water, bricks, cement, and all the necessary materials for the construction of so grand a work.

The second thing which surprised me, is, that this wall does not continue in the same line, but bends in divers places, following the line of the mountains in such a manner that, in lieu of one wall, one may say that there are three, which surround all this great part of China.

After all, the monarch who, in our days, has reunited the Chinese and Tartars under the same dominion, has done things more advantageous for the safety of China, than the Chinese emperor who built this long wall; for after having reduced the Western Tartars, partly by artifice, partly by force of arms, he obliged them to go and live three hundred miles beyond the Wall of China ; and in this place he distributed to them their lands and pasturage, while he gave their country to the Tartars his subjects, who live there at the present time. Meanwhile the Western Tartars are so powerful, that, if they agreed among themselves, they could yet render themselves masters of all China and Eastern Tartary, as the Eastern Tartars themselves acknowledge.

I have said that this monarch used art to subdue the Western Tartars ; for one of his first cares was by presents and demonstrations of friendship to engage the Lamas in his interest. As these false priests have great credit with the nation, they easily persuaded them to submit to the dominion of so great a prince ; and it is in consideration of this service rendered to the state, that the emperor looks still upon these Lamas with a favourable eye, that he gives them presents, and that he makes use of them to keep the Tartars in obedience, though in his heart he has nothing but contempt for their persons, regarding them as coarse men, without any knowledge of science or the fine arts ; by this some judgment may be formed of the wisdom and ability of this prince.

He has divided this vast extent of country into forty-eight provinces, which are submissive and tributary to him. It is astonishing that he alone should govern an empire of such vast extent, and that he is the soul which gives motion to all the members of this great body. Not only does he not suffer public affairs to rest upon any of his grandees, but he will never allow the eunuchs of the palace, or any of the lords of the court, who have been raised to be near himself, to dispose of anything within his house, or regulate anything of themselves. He takes notice of all affairs treated of in the courts of justice, and causes an exact account to be rendered of the judgments which are passed there. In a word, he disposes and orders everything himself ; and it is on account of the absolute authority which he has thus acquired that the greatest lords of the court, and the most distinguished persons in the empire, even the princes of the blood, always appear in his presence with the profoundest respect. He also shows most praiseworthy justice in punishing them, just as he does the humblest of his subjects, when they are guilty of any faults which deserve it.

For the rest, the Lamas, of whom I am going to speak, are not only respected by the people of their nation, but also their lords and princes, who show them much friendship ; and this makes us fear that the Christian religion will not find an easy entrance into Western Tartary.   They have also much power over the mind of the queen mother, who is of their country, and is seventy years old.   They often tell her that the sect to which she belongs has no enemies more de- cided than we ; and it is a kind of miracle, or at least a special providence of God, that, notwithstanding this, the emperor, who has great regard and respect for her, has not ceased to load us with honours and favour, regarding us always in a very different light to what these Lamas do.

During the journey, as the princes and the first officers of the army went often to the queen to pay her their court, and we were advised to do it likewise, we wished first to consult one of our friends among the grandees, who in the various occurrences which concern us speaks for us to the emperor. This lord went into the tent of the prince, and consulted him upon the subject ; he came out soon and said, " The emperor has told me, that it is not necessary for you to go and see the queen as the others do "; by which we well understood that this princess was not favourable to us.

The third reason which the emperor had for making this journey was his health : for he knows by long experience, that when he is too long in Pekin, he is sure to be seized with a variety of complaints, which he avoids by means of these long huntings. For all the time they last he sees no woman ; and it is very surprising that none appeared in all this great army, excepting those which formed the suite of the queen- mother, and it is an unusual thing that she accompanied the king this year, for it only happened so once before, when he brought the three queens with him as far as the capital city of Leauton to visit the sepulchres of his ancestors.

The emperor and the queen-mother expected by this journey to avoid the excessive heats which are felt at Pekin in summer during the dog days. For in this part of Tartary, until the months of July and August, there blows a wind so cold, particularly during the night, that it is necessary to wear warm clothing. The reason given for this extraordinary cold is, that this region is very elevated, and full of mountains. There was one among others which we always ascended during five or six days of March. The emperor wished to know how much it was above the plains of Pekin, distant from hence about three hundred miles; at our return, after having measured the height of more than one hundred mountains which were in our route, we found that they were three thousand geometrical feet above the level of the sea nearest to Pekin.

The saltpetre with which these countries abound, may also contribute to this great cold, which is so violent that in digging the ground to three or four feet deep they take out clods quite frozen, as well as pieces of ice.

Several petty kings of Western Tartary came from all directions three hundred and even five hundred miles, with their children, to salute the emperor. These princes, who for the most part know only their native language, which is very different from that spoken in Eastern Tartary, regarded us with looks and gestures of especial kindness. There were some among them who had made the journey to Pekin to see the court, and who had seen our church.

One or two days before arriving at the mountain, which was the limit of our journey, we met one of these petty kings, a very old man, who came to see the emperor. When he saw us, he stopped with all his suite, and asked by his interpreter which of us was called " Nauhauaii ".[1]   One of our

---

[1] This is misspelt in the French for Nanhauaij : but the proper form of the Chinese name given to Verbiest is Nan-hwae-jin, as is shown in his Chinese map of the world in the British Museum, where the name is given in the Chinese character.

servants having signified that it was I, this prince addressed
me with much courtesy, and said to me that he had known
my name a long time, and that he desired to know me. He
spoke to Father Grimaldi with the same marks of affection.
The favourable welcome we received in this meeting, gave
us some ground of hope that our religion might be received
by some of these princes, particularly if care were taken to
instil it into their minds through the medium of mathematics.
So that if it were contemplated at some future day to pene-
trate into their country, the surest way for many reasons,
which I have not leisure to explain here, would be to commence with the most distant Tartars, who have not submitted
to the empire, then pass on to those who have, and thus
advance gradually towards China.

During the whole journey the emperor has continued to
give us singular marks of good will, granting us favours in
the sight of his army which he bestows on no one else.

One day he met us in a large valley, where we were measuring the height and distance of some mountains ; he stopped
with all the court, and calling us from a distance, said in
Chinese, " Hao mo ?" which means " Are you well." Then
he put many questions in the Tartar language about the
height of the mountains, to which I also replied in the same
language. After that he turned to the lords who surrounded
him, and spoke to them of us in the most gratifying terms,
as I learned the same evening from the prince his uncle, who
was then at his side.

He has also shown us his affection, in often sending meats
from his own table to our tent, even desiring at certain meet-
ings that we should eat in his own : and always when he
has done us this honour, he has shown consideration for our
days of abstinence and fasting, sending us only such viands
as we might take.

The eldest son of the emperor, after his father's example,
has also shown us much kindness ; for when he was obliged

on one occasion to remain quiet for more than ten days, in consequence of a fall from his horse, which wounded his right shoulder, and a part of the army in which we were was in attendance on him, the emperor meanwhile following the chase with the remainder, he did not fail during all this time to give us every day some marks of good will, the which, as well as those which the emperor his father has loaded upon us, we regard as the acts of a special Providence, which watches over us and over Christianity.

It may be seen in different places in these letters, that the emperor of China is as good as he is great and powerful. He showed this to his people some years since in a remarkable manner. The city of Pekin and its environs were afflicted for three months with an earthquake, so horrible and violent at certain hours, that an infinite number of temples and palaces were cast down. The walls of the city fell, and more than four hundred persons were crushed. In a village named Tuncheu, thirty thousand inhabitants were buried under the ruins of their houses. The danger was so great for every one, no building being safe, that the emperor and all the court betook themselves to an encampment, and the people who had not the means of having tents, took the resolution of lying down in the open air. When the earthquake had passed off, those whose houses had fallen found themselves under the necessity of continuing this manner of life a long time, it being still more difficult for them to build a house than to have a tent ; and that which redoubled the public affliction was, that the most part had not the means of rendering the last duties to their relations, which the Chinese consider as one of the greatest evils of life. The emperor could not see the misery of his people without being moved with compassion. He resolved to relieve them, and behaved so generously to them, that he gave them money from his treasury, not only to build the houses of the living, but even to make the coffins of the dead.

In order to understand that part of the last letter which ^{Of the Lamas.} treats of the lamas, care must be taken not to confound them with the bonzes. The lamas are the priests of the idolatrous Tartars, and the bonzes those of the Chinese. The latter are held in great contempt in China among all people of condition ; and the former, as it is said in the letter, are venerated throughout Tartary, even by the grandees. The bonzes also are men taken from the dregs of the people, a collection of fellows who for the most part are great rascals : but the Lamas have among them people of quality, and it is not long since they had for their pontiff the brother of the king of Thibet. Above all they appear generally to live with the utmost regularity.

But in order to explain more thoroughly all that regards these Tartar priests, so often mentioned in the histories of China, and always taking too great a part in the affairs of this kingdom, I will relate here that which a Jesuit of Persia learnt respecting them from an Armenian priest, who had been in Thibet, and of another traveller of the same nation, a wise man of good faith, who had lived there four years, and whose recital deserves the more credit that the Father Gruber, who passed through there in coming to China, agrees with him perfectly.

There are two kingdoms in Asia which bear the name of Thibet. The one called the Little, the other the Great. The Little Thibet joins the kingdom of Cashmere, which is that beautiful country belonging to the Mogol, described by M. Bernier[1] as abounding in all kinds of fruits, like the most fertile provinces of Europe, embellished everywhere with gardens and watered by rivers of clear water, and inhabited by a race that is gentle, sociable, and hospitable to foreigners. The Little Thibet is quite the contrary as to the nature of

---

[1] The celebrated traveller François Bernier, who resided twelve years in India, during eight years of which he was physician to Aureng Zeyb.

the country : for it has a sterile soil, a cold climate, and the people are very poor.

The Great Thibet, which some call Tefat, and others Boutant, borders on Chinese Tartary. It is not much more agreeable and fertile than the Little Thibet. In general the people make no bread. Barley meal mixed with tea, which comes from China, or with some other liquor, serves them instead. Some nevertheless make barley bread. Most of the poor people eat their bread raw. The rivers supply them with very fine fish, and they have abundance of milk food. The soil produces neither wine nor fruit. They make pretty strong brandy from barley and other grains. They make use of the little wheat which they grow, to make other nourishing liquors.

Thibet abounds in musk. It is a wild animal, the colour of a deer, a little larger and longer than a cat, having two very large teeth in the upper jaw. Its perfume is at the navel. Hunting this animal constitutes the most common sport of the country. There are plenty of mines of gold and silver, but as the inhabitants do not know how to work the mines, the metals are only found by digging the ground at hazard, but this does not prevent their being sufficiently plentiful.

The air is excellent, and they are very seldom ill. The men are robust, fair enough in their dealings, and punish thieves very severely. Constancy in wedlock is strictly observed : but the unmarried live in great license. They do not bury the dead, but expose them to the beasts and birds, thinking it better they should be thus eaten, than become corrupt and furnish food for worms.

Lassa, which is the capital and only city of the country, is governed by a mandarin of China, sent there by the emperor, to whom this country is subject : from which one may judge of the immense extent of the Chinese empire, it being more than three months' journey from Thibet to Selink, a city situated at the foot of the great wall. Though the space between is a desert, where there is nothing but wild beasts, caravans frequently pass from Thibet to China, the capital of which is distant only two months' journey from Selink.

Besides the mandarin who governs in Thibet for the emperor of China, they have also, under the authority of the same monarch, a Calmuck prince, who has a separate jurisdiction, and to whom they give the title of king.

But it may be said, that the greatest lord in the country is the pontiff of the lamas, who is called the Grand Lamas, or the Grand Lam, or the Grand Lamasem, and who is certainly the famous Prestor John, who has, without foundation, been placed by some in Ethiopia. They have so much veneration for this Grand Lamas, that they regard him as a divinity : of whom these people acknowledge three. They say there is an invisible god, who never speaks to any one. Another, who is the word of god, and who communicates it to the Lamas ; and the third is the Lamas himself, who announces the word of god to others. The dwelling of this false priest is in a kind of fortress, a quarter of a league from the capital, and of the same name as the capital itself, where he governs 14,000 Lamas. There are two other fortresses, which are distant from hence several days' journeys, in one of which there are 12,000 lamas, and in the other 8,000, all under the command of the Grand Lamas, who disposes of them as he pleases, and who sends large troops of them as missionaries into Tartary and into China, without supplying them with food for their journey, or any other means of subsistence.

These lamas do not marry, but have among them certain communities of both sexes, which live more austerely than the others. They all, however, live very strictly, for they have fasts, mental prayers, a Lent of forty days, and other like penances. They have also a choir, and a kind of chant. Their temple is very magnificent, where are to be seen the statues of Adam and Eve. Father Gruber says, they offer a sacrifice of bread and wine, when they can get it.

This imitation of the practices of Christianity, has caused the Mahometans, who know them, to say that they are the infidels of the Christian religion. M. Thevenot believes that the Nestorians of Moussol and its environs formerly introduced the gospel into this country and even into China, and that these lamas are the remains of this Christianity, gradually corrupted by ignorance and by time. An illustrious and learned cardinal, to whom M. Thevenot gave his reasons for thus thinking, confirmed him by his approbation, which is a sure precedent for that of the public.

The Grand Lamas is extremely rich. It is he who gives permission to dig the earth to find gold, and whether they find it or not, the permission is equally valuable to him. As the country abounds in horses, camels, and other beasts of burden, he has a prodigious number of them. The credulity of the people is even a better revenue for him than all this. For everyone gives him something, and in acknowledgement of all the presents he receives, he has only to give them little reliquaries of brass, filled with all sorts of odd things, and these poor souls carry them about with them as a remedy for all kinds of evil.

It is not only the common people who suffer themselves to be deceived by this imposture, but the most considerable people of the country, over whom he has such an ascendancy that they do nothing but at his discretion. The governor and the king of Thibet are the first dupes of the false lights, which he pretends to receive from above. It is difficult to believe how blindly the princess, who is called in China the queen-mother, is devoted to all the superstitions of these false prophets. All her court is full of lamas, and she is so infatuated that she shares with them everything which she possesses. It is they who have made her an enemy of Christianity and the Christians, against whom she has an implacable hatred. The fortune of this woman is extraordinary; for she is not mother to the late emperor, and only grandmother to this by adoption. She had been the nurse of the former, who was so attached to her that he constantly showed her all the tenderness and deference which a son of the best natural disposition in the world could show to her from whom he had received his life. What is still more astonishing is, that the present emperor discovers the same dispositions towards her. In this manner she has been for a long time much looked up to in China, enjoying all the honours of a great queen, and even taking part in the affairs of government.

It may be considered as the greatest work accomplished by the ministers of the gospel who have had influence in this court, and one of the most essential services which they have been able to render to the cause of religion, that they have removed in the two conquerors the esteem which their ancestors had for the lamas : for it is no small proof of the moral courage of these monarchs, that they were able to raise themselves above this hereditary superstition. Whilst the passions of Chunchi left him the free use of his reason, he followed in this the counsels of father Adam ; and if for political reasons he took some steps for the honour of the lamas, he made them with dignity and due regard for his own character. At the commencement of his reign the high priest came to see him, in the hope of establishing himself director of his conscience, and perhaps minister of his empire. He came accompanied by three thousand of his people, clad in the red dresses which they all wear ; passing among the Tartars in this attire, they attracted to their train more than thirty thousand persons, together forming a magnificent cortege. One of the uncles of the emperor persuaded him to advance as far as the great wall, to receive so large a host at the entrance of his territory ; and the prince, who was quite young, had already made preparations for the journey, when father Adam, who had been warned of it, went to him and represented to him how much such an action would compromise the dignity of his empire. This remonstrance was effectual—the emperor acquiesced. The lamas came, and he received him well, but without servility or superstitious reverence. It is said that this man showed much address at this meeting, and that having enquired on the road in whom the prince had confidence, and who was his adviser, and being told that it was a foreigner from Europe, a man of ability and intelligence, he highly approved of the choice, and praised the good taste of the monarch.

The present emperor walks in the same steps, and what is still better, does not seem in danger of losing his mind like his father, women having less power over him. It is not that he has ceased to love them; if he had, he would have surmounted one of the greatest obstacles to his becoming Christian: but he loves them in such a manner, that if he is weak enough to make them mistresses of his heart, he has strength enough to prevent their empire extending over his reason, and in settling the affairs of his state the king does not become the slave. So that whatever attachment the queen-mother may have for the lamas, and however infatuated his best beloved women may be, he has always had esteem and affection for the Jesuits of his court, to whom, since he has known them, he has not ceased to show favour, and to give striking proofs of his royal good will.

This is for the consideration of those who shut their eyes to the progress made by the Christian religion in China, which is greater under the reign of this prince than one had dared to hope. Hitherto he has not manifested any disposition to embrace it. He argues upon it, and, as he has a fine mind, he acknowledges its beauty, and has often said that it teaches nothing contrary to reason. One day, having gone to see the fathers, he gave them a writing in his own hand, bearing these words, "I revere heaven"; which all the missionaries of China have placed in front of their churches, as a tacit approbation given by the emperor to the true religion: but he stopped there, and it was a false report at Moscow which said, that in the last encounter of the Muscovites and Chinese, this prince had written to the grand dukes, saying that he would not make war with them, because he knew and worshipped the same JESUS CHRIST whom they adored. We received last month a letter from China, which reached Europe in ten months, and which says positively the contrary, and asserts that this prince has not yet given the preachers of the gospel any hope of conversion. He would naturally be inclined to require the observance of his own edict, which forbids the making converts to Christianity, but permits those who have already become so the exercise of their religion. Several times the fathers at Pekin, thinking they had found a favourable opportunity, wished to ask the revision of this edict, and the withdrawal of a clause so dishonourable to Christianity. At last, to do nothing unadvisedly, they consulted an uncle of the emperor's, who is one of their best friends: " Do nothing," replied the prince to them, " make no stir in the matter. The emperor knows what is going on, and is not ignorant that in Pekin alone you annually make two thousand Christians : but he pretends to know nothing of it, and it would not be safe to attempt to make him change his line of conduct." This shews what wisdom is required to hold one's zeal in check in China, and what wrong is done to religion by those who, even with good intentions, bring hither any but such as are regulated by prudence and purified by charity. But this shows at the same time the condescension of this prince to those whom he honours with his friendship. We received some months since letters from one of our missionaries, in which, besides the details of what had been done in this mission, of which I do not here speak, he relates many instances of the kindness of the emperor to them. As they will serve to make known this monarch, whose portrait I have undertaken to make, I think I ought not to suppress things so useful for my purpose. They show how affable, gentle, con-

siderate, and even polite he is, and that few of the princes of
Europe know better how to add to the benefits they confer
by gracious words and manners. Thus writes the father.

The favours which we have received from the emperor are
so extraordinary, that even the grandees of the court would
consider themselves honoured by them. The fathers of Pekin
who are near to him, have received the greater part. He
sees them with pleasure, he speaks to them, he converses
with them for hours with the greatest familiarity. As he
is always addressed kneeling, not wishing that they should
remain so long in so inconvenient a posture, he has the
kindness to cause them to be seated.

In his travels, which are frequent, he takes them almost
always with him, and orders some one of the great officers of
his house to take charge of them. Two years since he took
the fathers Verbiest and Grimaldi into Western Tartary;
this year he has taken father Pereira,[1] to learn of him European music while on the road.

He has ordered that these fathers should learn the Tartar
language, and has himself chosen a master for them. He
knows Tartar and Chinese, but he likes the Tartar best, and
for this reason the fathers have applied themselves closely to
learn it. He now takes great pleasure in hearing them speak
and talking with them.

When they are sick he sends to visit them, and if they die
he takes upon himself the charge of ordering their funerals,
which in China is one of the greatest marks of friendship
that can be shown. It is his wish, nevertheless, that all the
ceremonies of Christianity should be therein observed; so
that more than once we have seen their bodies carried from
the house which they had occupied near the palace, through
the whole length of Pekin, a space of more than two leagues,

---

[1] A translation of Father Pereira's letter, describing his journey,
which is inserted by Witzen in his "Noord en Oost Tartarien," is given
at the end of this volume as an Appendix.

to a distant place of sepulture, with the cross elevated, and more than two thousand Christians walking two and two with wax tapers in their hands, as orderly as it would be done in the most Catholic city of Europe. It is the custom of the emperors of China, when they wish to do honour to the memory of any one, to send to his tomb an eulogium of four letters, written by their own hand, which they call a *yupien*. The highest grandees regard this as an honour, and it has sometimes occurred that the king of Tonquin, on sending to the emperor to request the investiture of his kingdom, has taken it as a great favour that that prince has given him one for his father, the late king. The emperor has bestowed this honour upon all the priests who have died at Pekin, and has even extended this favour into the provinces, having sent one to the funeral of a German father, named Christian Herdric, who died at Kiancheu, in the province of Chansi.

This eulogium came very à-propos as a reparation for the dishonour which religion received in the place where he died; for being alone, and having no priest near him, he remained in his coffin, without any one coming to perform the funeral ceremony. The idolators had already begun to insult the Christians, and begged them to return to their ancient religion, in which funereal duties, which among them are regarded as in the highest degree important and essential, are carefully performed towards the dead. There was even one mandarin in a neighbouring village, who had already begun to persecute them upon this subject, and had caused some of them to be beaten in order to make them leave a sect, which was considered impious; but he was greatly surprised when on a sudden, and when they least expected it, father Grimaldi appeared with a mandarin from the court, bearing in great ceremony the eulogium of which I have spoken, covered with a piece of yellow silk, that being the emperor's colour. This eulogium, and the pomp of the funeral which the emperor had ordered, restored honour and

13

tranquillity to this afflicted Church. As all the mandarins of the neighbourhood were present at the ceremony, the persecutor whom I have alluded to was obliged to be there too. He was in great apprehension as to the consequences of the violence he had shown; but he was reassured when the father, prudently concealing his knowledge of what had passed, confined himself to complaining of some idolators of his jurisdiction, who, contrary to the wishes of the emperor, disturbed the peace of the Christians. The mandarin, extremely glad to see the turn the matter took, promised the father that he would see the affair set to rights, and so they parted good friends.

Wherever the emperor passes on his journeys, he offers warm greetings to any of these fathers that he meets on the road. At the close of last year he went into the province of Chanton, to visit the sepulchre of Confucius, that celebrated philosopher of China, whose works have just been printed in France. As he passed by Cinan, where there is a church, he sent a mandarin to ask if there were any news of father Vallat, who is a French Jesuit presiding over the church, but who was then absent. Thence he went to Nanquin, where one of the first things that he asked of the mandarins who went before him, was where the church was situated. He expected that the fathers who have charge of it would come to salute him as the others did, but they did not dare to do so without being summoned. The emperor waited for them two days, till at length becoming impatient at their absence, he sent to them a mandarin of his household named Chao, a zealous friend of the fathers of Pekin, to reproach them with not having come to see him, and courteously to ask them if they had any complaint against him. The fathers replied, that the respect which they felt towards his majesty, had prevented them from presenting themselves before him, without knowing that it would be agreeable to him that they should do so. " *You ought to have had no doubt about it,*" replied the mandarin. " The emperor on his road to Cinan has first sent to call upon you ; how is it that no one has appeared to receive him ?" The father Gabiani, to whom he spoke, told him that the father who resided at Cinan was come to Nanking upon business, and that he was still there at that time. Upon which it was concluded that they should both go to do reverence to the emperor. They went, and were received with every mark of esteem and affection that they could wish. They made him some presents, according to the custom of the country, of which he retained some white candles only, they being a rarity and much valued in China. He on his part presented them with some gifts, but not of any particular value, for the Chinese emperors give very little, the object of their giving being rather to confer honour than wealth. He conversed a long time with them, and put various questions to them. On asking them at last if they had not some image of Jesus Christ about them, father Gabiani presented him a cross, which he took and examined, and then returned it to him. He made Chao tell them that he wished the fathers of Pekin to be informed of his visit. Chao informed them also that the emperor on his return would pass before the door of their house. They made preparations to receive him, and the reception which they gave him seemed very agreeable to him, particularly certain quatrains of seven syllables, in Chinese verse, that a young man who had been received into our company had composed in honour of him. The emperor read them attentively, and not satisfied with reading them, wished to take them away. All the fathers of Pekin came as far as one of his pleasure-houses, which was at three leagues distance from the city, to present themselves before him ; and when they were informed of all the kindnesses he had shown to their brethren, father Ferdinand threw himself at his feet, and thanking him in the name of them all said, " The great number of benefits, sire, thus daily heaped by your majesty upon us poor strangers, deprives us of

the power of expressing our gratitude for them. We are unable
to serve your majesty except by our prayers and good wishes,
and we have no means of repaying the eternal obligations
under which you have laid us, except by imploring the
sovereign monarch of heaven and earth to continue to pour
upon your majesty those blessings which have hitherto
rendered your reign the happiest and most flourishing that
the empire of China has ever seen." These words, spoken
in a manner which made the heart of the speaker appear
upon his lips, touched the emperor extremely, and the conversation which he then held with the fathers respecting their
churches, showed them that their gratitude had produced an
extraordinary impression upon him.

It was but shortly after this, that a plan presented itself to
their minds, from which we have reason to hope for a more
solid establishment than ever of the Christian religion in this
empire. This prince, taking into consideration that father
Verbiest was now aged, and that if he should die he would
only have two mathematicians left, asked him by what
means he might have six others, and if none had come from
Europe to Macao. The father answered him that there was
only one. The emperor replied, that he very much wished
there had been more, but at all events that one must be sent
for, and that one of the three should go to fetch him. Upon
which he pressed the father to name to him the one that he
thought best fitted for the journey, and the father excusing
himself, so that he might leave the selection to his majesty,
he chose the father Grimaldi, and gave him two mandarins
to accompany him.

This journey was very serviceable to the cause of religion
in these provinces, which were so remote from the court,
where the infidel mandarins are less checked from disturb-
ing the peace of the ministers of the gospel than in those
which are near the prince. The missionaries of different
religious orders which have churches in the province of

Canton, had recourse to the father to have a stop put to such annoyances, and he did deliver them from them. After which, continuing his journey he came to Macao, where he took the father whom he came to fetch, and returned with him to the court. The emperor received them both with his usual kindness, but not being yet satisfied with this small number of learned persons that he had drawn around him, he resolved upon sending the same priest back again, with orders to go into Europe to fetch him some mathematicians. We have just received the news that this missionary left Macao nearly a year ago. His arrival here and return to China, are looked forward to with impatience. The emperor, however, will soon have less reason to be anxious about his return, when the mathematicians which the king has selected for him shall have arrived at his court. They would have been there by this time if their voyage last year had been more fortunate, and if a bad ship had not compelled them, after making a great part of their way, to return to Siam, where they had embarked.

The skill of these learned men will not be that which will most interest the monarch to whom they are sent. The history of him who sends them, will appear to him more worthy of his curiosity, than all the secrets of their mathematics. The detail of so many great actions, which fame has carried but confusedly into those remote regions, being related to him by people who have been eye witnesses thereof, will give him more pleasure than all the curiosities of Europe. As he has a taste for virtue of all kinds, nothing in this prince will escape without his duly appreciating it. The rapid course of so many victories, the splendid and important conquests, the vast number of conquered enemies, are points in connexion with our monarch upon which all the world looks with the same eyes, and I venture to say also that that is not what will most keenly interest the great emperor of whom I speak. With a more delicate discernment, he will leave to others to admire the hero and the conqueror, that he may bestow his praises on a king who can do everything, but wills only that which is just, who has conquered only that which was his own ; whom neither his own advantages nor the weakness of his enemies have been able to tempt to push his conquests beyond his just rights, always ready to grant peace among the greatest successes of war, and showing a moderation, which is the more admirable in prosperity, that it has not been taught him by adversity.   This is what will be thought by a monarch who knows how to value virtue. Happy if in esteeming the virtue of the king, he have the courage to embrace our religion.   This is the object of our great prince, but *it is not given to him that willeth nor to him that runneth, but to him on whom God hath mercy.*

APPENDIX.

Translation of Father Ferdinand Verbiest's first letter from the Dutch. See Witzen's " Noord en Oost Tartarien," Vol. 1, p. 185.

AT the beginning of the present year 1682, the emperor of China made a journey into Eastern Tartary, after having put to death three rebel princes, and thus quelled an insurrection which had broken out in certain provinces of the empire. One of these princes was strangled in the province of which he had made himself master. The second was brought to Pekin, with the principal subordinate ringleaders, and cut to pieces in the presence of the whole court. The principal mandarins, whose parents and kinsmen had been murdered by the rebels, gave their assistance as executioners, and, with sabre in hand, satiated their vengeance with the blood of their victims. The third, however, who had been the principal leader of the rebellion, had already, by hanging himself, put a termination at once to his own life and to the seven years' tragedy of the war.

When the empire of China had thus been restored to peace, and the provinces were again in quiet enjoyment of their ancient liberties, the emperor, on the 23rd of March, undertook a journey to the province called Leauton, the birthplace and ancient abode of his ancestors, with intent to visit their places of sepulture, and to honour the same with the accustomed ceremonies: as also to visit and inspect in

Account of a journey of the emperor into Eastern Tartary.

person the extreme frontier of that part of his dominion toward East Tartary or Niuche, distant some one thousand one hundred Italian miles, of a thousand paces each, measured from Pekin to the boundary posts.

The emperor himself rode in advance on horseback, and next to him followed the prince, his son, ten years of age, who had for some years past been declared the heir of this so vast an empire. After these came three principal queens, each in a gilded carriage, and thereafter all the chief princes, the grandees of the entire court, and the principal mandarins of all ranks, all of whom were attended by many followers and appurtenances, and made up in all a number of some seventy thousand men.

It was the emperor's pleasure that I also should be attached to his suite on this expedition, and follow him everywhere; partly that I might with scientific instruments observe and note the atmospheric and terrestrial phenomena, the latitudes, the variation of the needle, and occasionally the height of mountains; and also that I might always be at hand to answer his majesty's questions as to celestial appearances, meteors, and such like. For which reasons he selected one of his officers, who was to provide for and superintend the safe conveyance on horseback of my instruments during the entire journey.

He committed me to the care of his uncle, who is also his father-in-law, and considered in all respects as the principal among the grandees of the empire, charging him to provide me with everything necessary for so long an expedition, the which in effect he, the uncle, executed to superfluity and with great kindness, admitting me to his own tent and table.

The emperor allotted to my use at all times ten or more horses from his own stable, and among them not a few which he had ridden and used himself, in order that I might have means of changing from one to another when the one I rode might be tired.

It was thus therefore that, at the cost of the emperor, and at none of my own, I performed the whole journey, upon which all the other mandarins were obliged to spend great sums from their own resources.

Our road lay uniformly in an easterly direction, and parallel with and near to it, on the left or northern side, runs a continuous chain of mountains, generally of considerable height, to the extreme east, a distance of more than a thousand miles. From the city of Pekin, indeed, to the entrance of the province of Leauton, a distance of two hundred and ninety miles, the road is level; but through the whole province, for about four hundred Italian miles, we encountered ridges of hill and mountain, which cost us time to ascend and descend. Finally, the remainder of our journey was generally along rough mountains, or through deep valleys; at times also were desert flats, two or three days' journey in extent, for five hundred miles further, till we reached a town called Ula, and a river called by the Tartars Songoro, and by the Chinese Sumpoa; and here was fixed and marked out the limits of our journey.

All the mountains, both in Leauton and beyond it towards the east, are covered with a growth of old oak and other trees, which for centuries have not felt the axe. For a space of several days' journey I passed through coppices of the hazel nut. I do not remember anywhere else to have seen such abundance of that kind of tree.

This entire district, especially beyond Leauton to the eastward, is mountainous. I have often, standing on a summit and looking round the whole horizon, discerned nothing but mountains and valleys, the haunts of tigers, bears, and other beasts of prey. Houses seldom met my view, except in some vale on the bank of a rivulet, and these were huts of clay and thatched with chaff or straw.

All the towns and villages, of which in Leauton I saw many, are completely ruined. One meets continually with

14

remnants of walls and heaps of rubbish. Among the ruins, however, not a few new dwellings have been raised here and there, and constructed without order, some of clay, others of rough stone, but the most of straw, and very few covered with tile or shingle.

Already, however, all traces have vanished of very many towns and villages which existed before the war; for so soon as the Tartar sovereign who excited the contest had collected a small force, he proceeded to recruit it on a large scale from all the towns; the latter he sedulously destroyed, in order to deprive his soldiers of all hope of a return to their homes. The capital, however, of the province of Leauton, called Yim-yam, is of considerable size and beauty, and no contemptible specimen of a royal residence. Its latitude, as I fixed it by more than one observation, is ninety-one deg. fifty-six minutes, that is, about two degrees higher than that of Pekin; which by all authorities, as well native as European, to this day is not considered higher than forty-one degrees. There is no variation of the needle in this capital, a fact which I ascertained by repeated trials. But in the town of Ula, situated at the extreme limit of our journey, in latitude forty-four degrees twenty minutes, the needle is deflected from the south to the west one degree and about forty minutes. To return, however, to our journey, from which we have somewhat digressed.

From the city of Pekin to the furthest east, and through the remotest districts, an entirely new road has been opened, for the purpose of enabling the emperor to travel it on horseback and the queens in their carriages. This road was conducted, to the breadth of ten feet, over hill and dale, and with bridges, over numerous rivers and rivulets, for more than one thousand Italian miles, and is as straight and even as circumstances would allow, the earth being thrown up on either side to the height of one foot, very neatly, as a kind of fence, and marked with posts at regular instances.

It was so smooth and well kept, that in fair weather especially it resembled a threshing-floor ; to maintain which condition persons were placed along its whole course, who suffered no one to travel it till after the emperor and queens had passed. Our Catholics in Europe scarcely take so much pains to smooth and beautify the road along which the Sacrament is conveyed on the high festival, as these people bestow on the pathway of their sovereign and his consorts, and this as often as he undertakes this journey from the capital. But another road, in all respects similar, is prepared for the return journey, the higher ridges of the hills being, as far as possible, levelled, and bridges thrown over every stream, on either side of which mats with painted dragons are hung out, like tapestry with us.

The emperor himself, for the most of the time, leaving the great road, betook himself to unbeaten paths through the mountains for the sake of the chase. Even when at times he travelled so as to keep company with the queens, he diverged from the high road so as to avoid spoiling it with the crowd of horsemen of his train. The emperor, I say, moved on thus a considerable space in advance. After him followed the gilded carriages of the queens with the imperial suite. Then came, at a convenient distance, the princes, grandees, and, finally, the mandarins, each according to his rank ; but the rear was closed up by innumerable bands of servants on horseback. Inasmuch as we fell in with no towns on the way which could lodge such a multitude, or provide it with necessaries, and the greater part of the way lay through desert districts (mountain and valley, as I have said), everything needful had to be carried with us. Innumerable carriages therefore, camels, mules, and horses, went on before, partly through by-ways, or followed, or, it may rather be said, accompanied us in one interminable procession, carrying tents, beds and bedding, cooking utensils, and such like. In addition to these were many troops of led horses, for the emperor, the princes, and nearly all the great men changed their horses frequently in a day's journey. Herds of oxen, flocks of sheep for daily slaughter, and swine, also accompanied us, driven across the country on either side ; and all this perpetual concourse of carriages, beasts, and men, although kept at some distance from the royal road reserved for the queens, nevertheless raised such a cloud of dust that we seemed to proceed in a perpetual mist; and frequently when the wind blew on our face or flank, we were unable to distinguish objects at fifteen or twenty paces distance.

Our stages were so marked out that our army reached every evening the course of some stream, and was able to construct its huts on the bank. At daybreak of every morning these were broken up, and the materials sent forward. By the evening, the officers in charge had selected a convenient site, in the first instance, for the encampment of the emperor and his consorts, and afterwards for the princes and mandarins, each in his place after the sequence of the eight blazons of the banners under which the Tartar war array of that people is distributed and ordered. After this fashion and order we performed, in some three months, with scarcely the intermission of a day's repose, the thousand Italian miles towards the east, and took the same time for our return.

When we arrived at the fortress called Yam-hay, which is situated partly on the narrow arm of the Southern Sea, and partly on the Northern Mountain, where the famous Chinese Wall separates the province of Leauton from that of Pekeli (this wall begins on the shore of the Southern Sea and runs for about five miles to the base of the highest Northern Mountain, and thence ascending the acclivity, is conducted over the topmost summits of other mountains far

away to the north-west) :—when, I say, we had passed the
wall, and were beyond the frontier of Leauton, the emperor, with the queens, grandees, and nearly all the mandarins, quitted the royal road and diverged to the left of it
(i.e., towards the North Mountains, which are connected
by a long ridge and terminate very far to the eastward), in
order to follow the chase henceforward every day. The
emperor then selected three thousand soldiers from those
who formed his body guard, and who were all armed with
bows and arrows. These spread themselves out on either
side round the mountain in a wide circle, the diameter of
which was at least three Italian miles. They were then
arranged in a certain order and distance from each other on
the circumference. In order to obviate any inequality or
break in the circle by some moving quickly and others
slowly, careful order was kept by officers, and among them
even some of the great men, who were distributed in the
circle. After the positions of all were arranged, each one
moved straight forward, whether the ground before him
were valley or thick underwood, or whether he had to climb
the most rugged heights, and none was allowed to diverge
to the right or the left.

And thus traversing hill and dale they surrounded all the
beasts within their circle as in a net, and gradually approaching a point, usually chosen in some valley free from trees,
they diminished the circle from one of a diameter of three
miles to one of two or three hundred paces. Then each dismounting from his horse (for the entire body of seventy
thousand men were horsemen, and there was not a pedestrian
among them), and setting foot to foot and shoulder to shoulder, they closed in upon the animals they had driven from
their dens and haunts. The latter, after running hither and
thither and finding no exit, sunk down powerless and exhausted and were easily captured. I have seen upwards of
three hundred harts, besides wolves, foxes, and other wild

animals, captured in this manner in the course of half a day. I have seen also, in the remoter districts of Tartary beyond Leauton, often more than a thousand harts and badgers taken in the same time, which, like flocks of sheep, running about the circle and finding no egress, fell a prey to their own exertions. Tigers, however, were, to the number of more than sixty, destroyed by another kind of proceeding and with different weapons.

It was the emperor's pleasure that I should be present at all these extraordinary hunts, and he recommended me to the care of his father-in-law, with special benevolence on my behalf, charging him to take particular care for my safety in the chase of the tiger and other dangerous beasts. It was thus that I alone among all the mandarins, without arms and near the person of the emperor, ascended on horseback the high mountains, and with him descended again into the valleys.

Returning thereafter after this severe labour (though, after a while, I got accustomed to it) late at night to the tents, I was usually so fatigued as scarcely to be able to stand after dismounting, and through the night was little conscious of the neighing of the horses, the lowing of the oxen, or the bleating of the sheep about our encampment.

And, albeit I often endeavoured to escape from this close company with the emperor, yet by advice of friends I was induced to give up the attempt for fear of his displeasure, inasmuch as he had exhibited an extraordinary inclination for me, yea, had distinctly expressed himself that I should always be about his person, like those who were in his most secret confidence and intimate friendship ; and all the great mandarins had conformed themselves to this the emperor's pleasure in my behalf.

After thus following the chase for a length of upwards of nine hundred miles, without a day's intermission, we reached at last the city of Xin-jam, where we enjoyed three or four days' repose. To this place came certain Coreans (from the peninsular of Corea), and brought to the emperor a living sea-calf, the which the emperor caused to be submitted to my inspection, asking me whether in our European books there were any mention of this fish ? And when I replied, that in our library at Pekin there was a book which contained a likeness and description of this fish, taken from life, the emperor desired that this book should be forthwith sent for. On my writing on this subject to the fathers at Pekin, I received in a few days their answer, together with two books, which the imperial messengers, by diverse conveyance so rapid as to resemble a flight through the air, delivered to me. When the delineation in these volumes and the description, were found to agree exactly with the specimen brought from Corea, the emperor was much delighted, and commanded the fish to be conveyed with great care to Pekin.

During the three days which we passed at this resting place, the emperor, with his consorts, visited the burial places of his grandfather and great-grandfather, which are not far from the city of Xin-yam.

On the fifth day he started, directing the queens to remain in the capital for the remainder of his intended journey beyond Leauton towards East Tartary, and, as before, following the chase without a day's intermission, and arrived finally, after traversing another four hundred miles, at a town called Kirin, placed on the shore of the great river Songoro, which has its source in the famous mountain called Cham Pè. This mountain is situated some four hundred miles to the south of Kirin, and is said to reach to the clouds, with its summit continually covered with snow. It is for this reason called by its name Cham Pè, which signifies white mountain. The foot or spur of this mountain is the ancestral birthplace of our Eastern Tartar race : the emperor, on this account, on the instant of his arrival on the river shore, dismounting from his horse, and with his face turned southward toward the mountain, knelt down and bowed his head three times to the earth, in honour of the mountain and its connexion with his forefathers. After this he mounted his litter resplendent with gold, and surrounded by his body guard he entered the town of Kirin. He let himself be seen by everyone, and forbad his guard to keep the multitude at a distance, as is the custom at Pekin; for the whole population, men and women, had poured out to meet him, with every indication of delight at the sight of their sovereign, and contemplating him as if he had descended from heaven : for it had never for ages past happened that the Chinese emperor had visited these provinces in person. The emperor was himself pleased at these unaffected demonstrations of loyalty on the part of his subjects. He laid aside all pomp of majesty, and invited their near approach, displaying towards them the simplicity of his ancestors.

In this town of Kirin the inhabitants build vessels of a peculiar construction, and keep a good many equipped, with which they navigate the river towards the north-east for some miles, and come to blows with the Muscovites, who often frequent these rivers and endeavour to take away the pearl fishery from the Kiringers.

After the emperor had enjoyed two days' repose at Kirin, he proceeded with upwards of two hundred vessels and some of his great men down the river to Ula, which is considered the most illustrious city of the whole province, and was of old the residence of the Tartar emperors, the ruins of whose palace are yet to be seen. He again took me in his company, leaving behind at Kirin all the princes whom the vessels were insufficient in number to accommodate. In this river, a little above Ula, which is situated on its shore, some thirty-two miles from Kirin, there is abundance of sturgeon. It was to take this fish that the emperor proceeded to Ula. It happened, however, that at this juncture, heavy rain fell day and night, and the river, without respect for his Majesty, rising and continuing to rise, became by the force of its current unmanageable, and frustrated the further progress of his Majesty.

The emperor remained here five or six days, for the rain fell incessantly, and finally compelled him to retrace his course back to Kirin. Upon this return one vessel suffered no little injury by the violence of the opposing current, and I and the emperor's father-in-law were obliged to disembark. We betook ourselves to a peasant's waggon drawn by one ox, and moving on slowly through thick mud and heavy rain, came at last, late at night, again to Kirin. When the emperor heard our adventure he said, laughing, " The sturgeon has made sport of us."

After two days' repose at Kirin, the rain having somewhat abated and more cheerful weather having set in, we commenced our journey back to the capital of Leauton. It is impossible in few words to describe the labour and difficulty of this journey, the constant rains of the previous days having made all the roads impracticable. For while we were compelled to traverse a mountainous country, the waters streaming down through every valley had swelled the streams, if I may so express myself, to an intolerable degree of arrogance, to the destruction of the bridges which had before existed.

The waters also had formed standing pools, with tenacious mud, in many of the valleys, covering many a fertile and verdant meadow. Among these the horses, camels, and other beasts of burthen, laden with the travelling apparatus, got bemired and exhausted. The way was crowded with corpses and remains of these animals, not merely of those which perished on their return, but also of those which had sunk on the advance. Scarcity also of provision (for many articles which we had taken with us were now deficient), began to tell on the spirits as well as the bodily strength of

15

the men. Many horsemen now dismounted and led their
horses. Many of the cattle drivers were also obliged to halt
for some days, in order to let their droves pasture and re-
fresh themselves. Many others had lost their horses altogether. Men sent on in advance in great numbers, with
much difficulty cleared the way of trees and brushwood. In
spite of this precaution some thousand horsemen and carriages, which had started long before daybreak on the
beaten road, lost it altogether from its impracticability. The
emperor himself and his little son, with all the great men of
their suite, were in many places compelled to wade on foot
through mud and water, fearing lest from a false step of their
horses on the bundles of faggots which lay concealed by the
mud, they might incur greater peril. On arriving at narrow
passes or bridges, which abounded in the valleys, after the
emperor and some of his nearest attendants had passed, there
ensued such a contest, I may say such a wrestling among
the multitude for the passage, that many tumbled over each
other into the water. In truth, for the whole of the way
through Tartary, and especially the eastern part, the difficulty and suffering were so excessive, that many who for
thirty years and more had followed the court, avowed that
they had never experienced the like.

In these difficult passages of narrow places, the emperor
gave various tokens of his good inclination towards myself.
On the first day of our homeward journey, we arrived
at a stream which was found so swollen as to be fairly and
utterly unfordable. The emperor then availed himself of a
small boat, which by mere chance was at hand, and first
took himself and the young prince over, and afterwards some
of the chief members of the imperial family; but when the
other princes, grandees, and mandarins, and the whole troop
of followers were crowding to the shore, and anxiously desired a passage (for dark night was at hand, and the tents
and all the travelling apparatus had been sent on and con-

veyed over two days in advance, and in consequence there was no choice but to cross at once or to pass the night without supper, and in the case of many without a dinner, on the bare earth, in a very cold season), the emperor returned across the stream and brought a second boat with him, and cried aloud : " Where is Nan Goay gim ?" (that is my name among these people), whereupon his father-in-law replied, " Here he is." The emperor rejoined, " Let him get into the boat and cross with ourselves ;" and thus caused me to cross over, leaving the others behind. And this transaction caused no little comment among the multitude of eminent persons, who, through the night and following day, were toiling to effect their passage.

It fell out in very like manner on the following day, for the emperor, with some of his principal nobles, to wit, such as had succeeded in crossing during the night, arriving about midday at a stream greater than the former, after from midday to sunset had been occupied with passing over the tents in small boats, he again ordered that I and a very few besides should be conveyed over, leaving all the others to pass the night on the other side. And when the emperor's father-in-law asked, through one of the chief intimates of the emperor, " whether he also was to cross, inasmuch," he added, "as Nan Goay gim shares my tent and table," the emperor replied : " It is necessary that you should cross, but as concerns Nan Goay gim, I shall provide for him with my own tents and table."

When I reached the other side, the emperor, sitting on the river bank, commanded me to sit by him, together with two sons of a prince of the Western province, and the chief Tartarian Kolao, to whom he always shewed much affection. The night being very clear, the emperor would have me recite the names of all the chief stars which he embraced in his view of the hemisphere, as well in the Chinese as in the European language, and he himself displayed all the knowledge which he had acquired on the subject. After he had produced a small chart of the stars, which I had some years before prepared for him, he went on to tell by the stars the hour of the night, and took pleasure in thus displaying his science in the presence and hearing of the great men about him.

These and other tokens of the imperial favour (as, for example, his frequently sending me meats from his own table) were so remarkable and notorious to all, that when the two uncles of the emperor, who were the chief of the grandees of the realm, visited me, upon our return to Pekin, at my residence, they said to the fathers who were with me : " So great is the affection of the emperor for Nan Lao Te" (this name they gave me as one of honour), " that when he is low in spirits he has only to look on Nan Lao Te, and he immediately recovers his cheerfulness." This exceeding favour of the emperor materially diminished the labour of our arduous journey, but I never could discover any special reason why I enjoyed it.

Having accomplished by such assistance the return journey (to make an end of details), I arrived on the 9th of June, late at night, safe and sound at Pekin. Many who had suffered injury on the road by falls from their horses, had been fain to turn back, and many attacked with illness had remained behind.

Some may here be disposed to ask, what advantage or profit could be derived to our mission from this expedition ? To which I reply,—first, that I could do no other than obey the emperor's express command that I should accompany him, for on the emperor's good will (humanly speaking), depend entirely the success and utility of our mission.

In the second place, upon the whole course of this journey (although by indirect ways), and in many of the most remote places, as in Xin-yam, the chief place in Leauton, situated on its frontier, in Kirin itself, and in Ula, which 1 may call the uttermost spot of the inhabited world, I met with some Christians whose confession I received, and others whom, already instructed by the former, I baptised, who but for the chance of such an opportunity could with difficulty have lighted on the means of salvation and holiness. And among these Christians were two invested with the Bachelor's degree, and another had long enjoyed that of Licentiate, all of whom resided in the celebrated town Caiyuen, within the province of Leauton.

I passed half a day in this town, leaving the great road for the purpose. Our constant advance permitted no longer stay.

In the third place, I found occasion on this long expedition to infuse many notions of Christian doctrine into many of the grandees and other mandarins, and to acquaint them with the object and nature of our mission, and of the spiritual order in Europe. For inasmuch as not only the nobles, but also the princes of the imperial family, to divert the tedium of the journey, courted conversation with me, and asked me many questions touching the heavens and the stars, and much about meteors, as also about our sea voyages, I took such opportunities to throw in much information as to our Christian doctrine and worship ; and I took special pains to point out how widely our religious missionaries, i.e., those from Europe, differ from the Chinese bonzes or priesthood, who occupy the lowest place in society. To wit, that the spiritual class in Europe, from their youth to extreme age, occupy themselves with every branch of letters and science : and also, after entering on their spiritual functions, become examiners of Bachelors and Licentiates, and are made secular Doctors, and thus in Europe rank with the mandarins, whom in China we call Hio Tao, that is, examiners of those who take degrees ; and all this I demonstrated by the European books full of science, which have been translated into Chinese and spread all over the country.

So that the greater number of the nobles and principal mandarins thus acquired an exalted notion of our European clergy, a knowledge which, but for the opportunity of this journey, they could hardly have obtained.

In the fourth place. Inasmuch as this countless multitude of men, who during the entire journey saw me mounted on one of the emperor's horses, and heard me from the same, as from a pulpit, often discourse of our worship, in such manner that I might be said to be preaching to an enormous congregation; for there were few among them who had not their attention turned to the emperor as he passed them from time to time, and who did not also see me in near attendance, distinguished as I was for the absence of bow and quiver, and by my long beard and European attire, they could not fail to observe me with close attention. As, moreover, nearly all knew me, not only as the author of the Chinese almanack, whose name by means of that book has been spread throughout the empire, but also as one who professed with singular zeal the doctrine of Christ; moreover as one who, after the overthrow and expulsion of Yam-quam-Sien, had reintroduced into China the European astronomy, together with the Christian doctrine; all this could not be without inducing many to ask questions touching the Christian faith, and, while some were one way inclined, some another, there arose much mention of the bygone persecution as well as of the present condition of the Christians. The result was, that they looked upon me as a principal and head among the latter, with the respect which they formerly shewed to father J. Adam Schal. And this respect was shewed by the fathers, who, by God's permission, co-operated with me in the pursuit of science, and whose names and titles being printed in the almanack, were in wide repute, not only as compilers of the same, but as apostles and champions of the Christian faith.

I append here a list of the places of East Tartary through which we passed by daytime, between the capital Leauton and Kirin, with the respective dates and distances. The names are given in the Tartar language, according to the usage of the places themselves.

Length of intervals between certain places on our line of route in East Tartary.

	Chinese Stadia.
1st day's journey from Xynyam, capital of Leauton, to Sea Ly Ho (this is a Chinese name) - -	95
2nd day, to the brook Chakay Anga - - -	85
3rd day, to another brook with the same name - -	70
4th day, to Kiaghuklen - - - -	50
5th day, to Feyter - - - -	80
6th day, to the brook Ciam - -	60
7th day, to the brook Seipery - - -	60
8th day, to a place Couroni - - -	50
9th day, to a place or village Sape - -	40
10th day, to a place Quaranny Pyra - - -	40
11th day, to Eltem Eme Ambayaga - - -	70
12th day, to Ypatan - - - -	58
13th day, to Suyen Nypyra - -	60
14th day, to Ylmen - -	70
15th day, to Seuten - -	70
16th day, to the town of Kirin - - -	70

In all, 1028 stadia, or 369 Italian miles. A Chinese stadium contains 360 geometrical paces, and 1000 of the same make an Italian mile : and four Italian miles make a common German mile. A geometrical pace contains five feet ; a common pace or step 1½ foot.

It were worth the trouble of some one with greater leisure than I can command, to make out from this list a travelling map, and to insert it into a map of the province of Leauton, which might easily be sketched out from the Atlas of father Martinus ; albeit some of the latitudes in the northern portion may require correction.

I shall here briefly add what I heard from some of the inhabitants of Ula ; to wit, that Hiucuta, or Niucuta, a place well known in that district, is distant seven hundred Chinese stadia from Ula, in a north-easterly, or rather more northerly direction.

The journey, however, from Hiacuta along the great river

Helung (into which flow the great river Sangoro and several other great streams), and down its waters towards east northeast, is one of about forty days, and then we reach the East Sea, at what I consider to be the Strait of Anian.

So much I was informed from his own mouth, by the chief military commandant who resided in Kirin, who had performed this journey, and had reached a sea subject to extreme cold.

[*The following occurs in Witsen in the form of a note, but without reference to any special part of the Letter.*]

Of the person of the Chinese emperor now reigning, the last Dutch ambassador at the Court of Pekin gives the following account in his diary.

The emperor is a man of moderate stature, gentle, sedate, venerable in demeanour, to be distinguished among a thousand apart from any exterior tokens of majesty but these, which consist in his own stately and polished deportment, and indicate the high qualities of his mind, in which he is not excelled by any prince or sovereign I have ever seen, and, at the least, vies with any such. He seems born to command, is conversant with many branches of science, to which he daily applies himself, as also to the affairs of his empire, which he has much at heart, devoting to them fixed hours both before and after noon.

This prince, in order to afford to all others an example of many virtues, requires nothing but the Christian faith, the which, from addiction to pleasurable indulgence, he is not likely to embrace, the propensity to plurality of wives being the main hindrance to its introduction among the great in China, who prefer their pleasure to all religious considerations ; so that, according to the Romish fathers, the gospel there is preached with effect only to the poor.

The now reigning emperor of the Tartar race, is said to be about fifty years of age ; of handsome exterior, has large black eyes, a somewhat elevated nose, with dark pendent whiskers (? moustaches), little or no beard, somewhat pitted in the face, and of moderate stature.

The Jesuit Le Comte, thus describes the Chinese emperor Camhi. " The emperor appeared to me of stature above the average, more corpulent than those among us who are proud of their shape, but a little less so than a Chinese desires to be ; the face full and marked with the small-pox ; the forehead large ; the nose and eyes small, like those of the Chinese ; the mouth handsome, and the lower part of the face very agreeable. His demeanour is benevolent, and one remarks in all his manners and actions, something which indicates the sovereign and is distinguished."

Letter of Father Ferdinand Verbiest, sent from Pekin, the capital of China, to Europe ; concerning a Second Journey which he made with the Emperor of China, beyond the great Chinese Wall into Tartary.

THE emperor of China, on the 6th of July, A.D. 1683, being the thirtieth year of his life, with the queen, his grandmother, and a great attendance, to the amount of 60,000 persons and 100,000 horses, commenced a journey to West Tartary, having expressed a special desire that I should accompany him, together with one of the two fathers my colleagues at my selection. I accordingly selected Philip Grimaldi, as being the older, and specially accomplished in the sciences. The causes of this journey were several. The first was, to keep the military during peace in constant movement and practice, to fit it for the exigencies of war. For this motive the emperor, in this same year (having made a levy from all his provinces of his best troops), returning to Pekin, after having established a solid peace throughout the vast empire of China, resolved in his council to make annually three such expeditions, each at a certain season, in the which he might, on the pretext of the chase and of practising his soldiers in the pursuit of stags, wild boars, and tigers, procure an image and representation of war with human enemies and rebels, and a rehearsal of conflicts which might thereafter ensue. He had in view at the least to prevent for his soldiers, and especially his Tartar troops, that infection of Chinese luxury and corruption which might otherwise naturally ensue from the idleness of peace. And, in fact, this

16

fashion in which the emperor went forth to the chase, had all
the form and appearance of a royal progress to war; for he
went attended by 100,000 horses and more than 60,000 men,
all armed with bow and arrows and sabre, and divided into
troops and companies, and with all the military accompani-
ments of banners and music. In the chase these surrounded
mountains and forests in a wide circuit, like those who invest
a town to be besieged; in which they observed the process
pursued by the Western Tartars in their great hunts. The
army, again, is divided into an advanced, a centre, and a
rear-guard, and into wings right and left. The command of
each of these bodies is committed to officers of eminence,
and to members of the imperial house.

Inasmuch, however, as this expedition was planned for a
march of more than seventy days (the emperor being on each
day from morning till evening devoted to the chase), and all
the provisions, and baggage, and other heavy impediments had
to be conveyed over continual ascents and descents, partly
on waggons, partly on camels, mules, and horses, the labours
and difficulties of each day's march are not to be described.
For in the whole of this West Tartary (West Tartary is not
to be understood as relative to China, which is itself west of
it, but with relation to the more Eastern Tartary) nothing is
met with but mountain and valley. It has no towns, and no
villages, no, not even a house. All its inhabitants live as
herdsmen under tents or hovels, which they convey from
valley to valley when they move in search of fresh and better
pasture for their herds, which consist solely of oxen, sheep,
and horses; for of pigs, dogs, geese, and other animals, which
abound among an agricultural peasantry, they have none.
I say that they possess nothing but these cattle, which graze
the uncultivated soil.

These Tartars are a slothful people, and little disposed to
any toil, even to that of the chase. They neither sow nor
reap, nor plough nor harrow. They live for the most part

on milk, cheese, and flesh. They make a certain wine which resembles our brandy, and which they delight to swallow to repletion, till they fling themselves down and are reduced, soul and body, to the condition of the very cattle.

They hold, meanwhile, their priests, called lamas, in great veneration, and in this respect are distinguished from some neighbouring Tartar tribes, who practise no religious observances, or next to none, and live as Atheists.

Both being equally slaves, and bound to the service of their lords, are on this account difficult of conversion to our faith ; following the nod of the latter, in matters of religion, like the cattle, which follow where they are led, not where they choose to go.

This part of Tartary, so far as it belongs to the Chinese emperor, is some thousand Chinese stadia, or about three hundred Italian miles in length, lying from south-east to north beyond the terrible great Wall of China.

In this manner did the emperor lead his troops a march of many days, through such desert districts, over ridges of mountains almost linked with each other, over many acclivities, beyond measure steep and far removed from the ordinary track. He followed the chase every day, riding in advance of the troops, often under a blazing sun, sometimes in heavy rain. Many who had taken part in the campaigns of preceding years, openly confessed to me that they had never, in actual war, endured such hardships as in this factitious campaign. Thus the emperor fully compassed his primary object, that of inuring his troops.

It appears, however, that another motive for the expedition was, the political object of keeping these Western Tartars in obedience, and checking the plots and intrigues of their councils. This was one reason for the magnitude of the force, and the imperial pomp with which the emperor penetrated their country. For this he conveyed also thither some pieces of cannon (to wit, those which I had cast for him of copper in former years at Pekin). These he occasionally caused to be discharged in the winding valleys, in which the reverberation from the cliffs added to the effect of those thundering salutes with which the emperor's movements from his palace in Pekin are usually attended; and which, as also the accompanying music of trumpets, drums, and copper cymbals, were now employed on the occasions of the emperor's marching, or at meal times, to dazzle and fill the eyes and ears of the barbarous tribes. For the Chinese empire has, from remote times, feared no enemy so much as these Tartars, who, starting from this Eastern district, encompass Northern and Western China with a countless multitude of tribes, to repel the invasion, or, so to speak, the inundation of which, former emperors constructed the great Wall. I had four times passed over and personally inspected that work. In truth, the seven wonders of the world condensed into one, could not be compared with it. That which I have seen with my own eyes of it, far exceeds all report of it which has yet reached Europe.

There are two circumstances which exalt this work to the skies. The first is, that it is carried not alone over level places, but in many places over the highest summits of the mountains from east to west, and follows all the acclivities; towers of a lasting construction rising high into the air, at intervals of two bow-shots apart. On our return we ascertained by our instruments the height of a portion of the Wall above the horizon at 1037 geometrical feet.

We might well wonder how the builders could draw to such a height, up the steepest places, from the lowest valleys, which are destitute themselves of water, such a quantity of stones, lime, water, etc.

The other circumstance is, that the Wall should be carried, not with one, but with a variety of curves, following all the prominences of the mountain; so that it may be considered not a single, but a triple Wall, which protects the whole Tartarian frontier of China.

APPENDIX. 125

It is certain that the first Tartar emperor of China and Tartary accomplished a better work for the protection of the Chinese empire than the Chinese emperor who built the Wall; for this farseeing sovereign after subjecting, partly by policy and partly by arms, all the Western Tartars, pushed on the boundary posts of the Chinese empire to more than three hundred Italian miles beyond the great Wall. All the intervening territory he distributed among his Eastern Tartars, who have now everywhere established farms and hamlets of their peasantry, though solitary and far distant from each other. But for this, if the Tartars acted in concert, it is thought they might overrun both China and East Tartary.

It is known that the first Tartar emperor subjected the West Tartars by policy and subtilty; for among other means which he employed were the priests, named lamas, whom he lured to his service by good offices and presents. These lamas being in great authority with the West Tartars, used it in the emperor's service.

For the same reason the emperor, who now rules both China and the two Tartaries, looks with an eye of favour on the lamas, and uses them to hold the Tartars in obedience, though he abhors them in his heart as men unclean and destitute of arts and sciences.

The emperor has divided the immeasurable districts of West Tartary into forty-eight provinces, and has made them all subject and tributary; and thus may this sovereign of the Chinese and of both Tartaries, be justly named as the greatest and mightiest monarch and sole ruler in the world; as one who has incorporated into one body so many districts and nations under one authority, without the interposition of any other prince. He may, I say, be named, as the monarch most essentially and most singularly worthy of the name, for this reason, that he of all rulers the most by himself governs so vast a multitude of men; for what is most remarkable in him and distinctive from all others, is that from the beginning of his

reign to this present day since he took the helm of government, he has never permitted any one to govern for him or
in his place, nor allowed any one, whether of the princes of
the realm, or of the kolaos, or other authorities who may be
familiar with him, or who enjoy his favour and are near his
heart, more than others to dispose of or settle any public matter by their own separate deliberation.   Nay, not within the
innermost recesses of the palace has he ever so condescended
to any of the eunuchs or the youth of the court, his cotem-
poraries with whom he had been brought up from infancy,
as to allow any one of them to act on his own behalf in
public matters ; facts which are altogether singular, and may
be regarded as miracles in this kind of government, when
the practice of his predecessors is taken into consideration.

This emperor chastises offenders of the highest as well as
lowest class with marvellous impartiality, according to their
misdeeds, depriving them of rank and dignity.   He himself,
after considering the proceedings and sentences of the Imperial Council or the Courts of Law, determines and directs
the issue.   On this account men of all ranks and dignities
whatsoever, even the nearest to him in blood, stand in his
presence with the deepest awe, and recognize him as sole
ruler.

As a point which concerns ourselves and our objects, I
must refer to my former observations on the Tartar priests
or lamas, that these, by reason of the policy pursued in the
government of the Tartaries, have easy access to the princes
and dignitaries, a circumstance which makes the introduction of our faith among these people the more difficult.
These priests have much influence with the queen-mother,
who sprung from West Tartary, and has attained the age of
fifty, and they have for many years past enjoyed her warm
affection.

Inasmuch as this queen is held in great consideration by
the emperor, and knows well from these priests that we are

strong opponents of the superstition to which she clings, it is a wonder, nay a miracle, at the least a singular proof of God's power and providence, that the emperor should have hitherto treated us with such benignity and with familiarity and honour, even beyond these lamas themselves.

Throughout this journey the tent of the queen-mother was much frequented by the great men and local authorities, who presented themselves to compliment her and inquire after her health; and as it was suggested to us to imitate their example, we consulted the confidential courtier through whom all our affairs with the emperor were conducted. This adviser having made the emperor acquainted with the case, returned immediately to us with the answer, " The emperor says that it is unnecessary that you should present yourselves in the queen's tent to pay your respects". We well understood from this that the queen was little inclined towards us.

The third and last cause of this expedition was that the emperor wished to consult the condition of his health ; for experience had taught him, that while he remained at Pekin his health from various annoyances often failed him, which he hoped by his present movement and change of life to provide against, and even to gain strength. For through the whole time devoted to this expedition he refrained from all intercourse with women ; and in that numerous multitude not a single woman was to be seen, except those who attended on the queen-mother. Even her presence was an accident, as was that in the year preceding, when he conveyed three queens to the capital of Niuche for the purpose of visiting the tombs of their ancestors in that place. For so often as in former years he had undertaken such expeditions, he had never taken a single woman with him.

It may be added that by this movement he with the queen-mother avoided the summer heat, which in the dog-days at Pekin is tremendous. For in this part of Tartary not only is the air very cooling, but wintry, especially at night, so that the inhabitants not only wear woollens, but betake themselves to furs and peltry for clothing. The cause of this is the mountainous character of the country and its elevation, such that for five days' journey we were constantly traversing high ridges, and climbing higher and higher.

The emperor desired to know how much this mountain was elevated above the level of Pekin, from which capital it is about three hundred miles distant, and commanded us to devise some means of measuring the difference. We therefore on our return, after measuring the heights and distances of more than one hundred summits, found that the horizon, or rather the circular level of Pekin was three thousand geometrical paces lower than the highest ridge or top of this mountain.

The soil in these highlands being much impregnated with nitre, may perhaps be a cause of this great cold. Wherever the earth is dug to the depth of three or four feet, this substance is turned up frozen like ice.

Several petty kings of West Tartary came in to see the emperor from distances of three and even five hundred Italian miles, with their sons and kinsmen. They all saluted us with great demonstration of good will, which they evinced openly by looks and gestures of hand and body. For many of them could speak no language but their own, which is different from that of the East Tartars. Some also had formerly been presented to us at Pekin, and some had visited our church there.

One day as we were arriving at the town which was the end and object of our journey, we met towards dusk a very old prince, who was returning from the emperor's tents, and on our appearance halted with all his attendants, which was very numerous, and asked, through an interpreter, which of us was Nau Hoay Gi? One of our followers pointing me out with voice and gesture, he approached us with much appearance of pleasure and benignity, and said, " I have long since heard of your name; are you well?" He approached father Grimaldi with the like demeanour, and asked how he was? From this conduct we derived some hope that at some time or other our worship might find access to these secular princes, especially should some of our scientific brethren find means to open the door of such access by pleasing exhibitions of knowledge, and if the people could be cajoled by presents.

As, however, this method requires time, it seems to me easier to begin with the more remote tribes, who dwell farther from the great wall, and who are not yet subject to the empire of China, and thus to work on by degrees to the other Tartars, and this for reasons which I can detail in small compass.

The emperor throughout our whole journey exhibited to us a benevolence and attention, such as, in truth, he displayed to no one else, not even of the princes or his own kinsmen, and this both in word and deed in presence of the whole army.

One day as the emperor fell in with us in an extensive valley, while we were employed in a scientific operation for ascertaining the height and distance of certain mountains, he halted with all his court and escort, and while still at some distance, shouted out in the Chinese tongue, " Hao mo?" that is, are you well? He then asked some questions in the Tartar language as to the heights of the mountains, which I answered in the same. He then turned to his attendants and spoke much in our praise, all which his uncle, who was present, reported to me that evening.

The same goodwill he showed us on many other occasions, to wit, in frequently sending us dishes from his own table to our tent, in the sight of all his grandees. He even ordered us sometimes to be entertained in his own tent. Sometimes when he knew we were abstaining from flesh, he would send us dishes suited to our wants. For he well knew

17

our habits of keeping fast days, and would often ask whether the day were a fast day or not.

His eldest son, following the example of his father, showed us similar goodwill. Once having hurt his shoulder by a fall from his horse, he was obliged to remain still for ten days, which we also did with the greater part of the army. On this occasion, his father being far absent with the chase, he almost every day, and often twice a-day, at midday and evening, sent to our huts dishes from his own table.

This constant benevolence of the emperor is so much the more to be ascribed to the special favour and providence of God, because to others, and even to the princes of his blood, he is very mutable and unstable in his disposition.

All the rest which concerns this journey much resembles that of the preceding year to Eastern Tartary, which I also performed, as I shall relate in following letters. To wit, how we were carried the whole way on horses or litters, and how we used the tents and table of the emperor's uncle, to whose care we were specially consigned. How, also, a great road was made over hill and dale for the convenience of the queen-mother, who travelled in a litter, for upwards of six hundred miles, going and returning, for we returned by a different way. Over the brooks, and over one in particular which had innumerable windings, bridges were everywhere constructed, and the ridges of the hills, even the most rocky, were levelled. It is scarcely credible to Europeans with what expense and labour this road was made.

Other incidents hereto belonging will be found related at length in the letters of Philip Grimaldi.

What were the fruits of our journeys, and what the advantage to Christendom, I have related in former years in my account of my journey into East Tartary. One observation on this head is sufficient. The will of the emperor was in all cases a limit to us. To oppose this, or to make any the slightest demonstration of doing so, would be to imperil at once our whole mission. I did, however, twice venture to confer with the principal courtier, through whom the emperor always communicated to us his commands or tokens of his favour, and twice, I say, requested him, if he could do it without hazard, to move the emperor to excuse us for the future from these journeys, or at least to leave me, advanced in years as I am, behind, at all events not to associate any two burthened with years in such a task.

On our furthest journey, at the greatest distance from Pekin, I have with sufficient punctuality received letters from our fathers at Pekin, and could always transmit answers when required. For along the whole road couriers of the nobles were constantly coming and going. And although this our march and journey was in show so dignified and illustrious, I can truly say of it that no missionary father in China has endured the hundredth part of the toil and hardship which we encountered in these journeys, whether with regard to the country or to the time occupied, or to other incidents. All which I cannot in any short compass describe. What I do relate has been noted with a hasty pen, on horseback, day by day. I request that it may be read with as cursory attention of eye and mind as that with which it has been written.

Pekin, Oct. 4th, 1683.

Narrative of a Hunting Excursion performed by the present Emperor of China, beyond the Great Wall, in the adjacent district of West Tartary, written by Father Pereira from his personal observation : from which the condition of these desert wastes may be in some measure apprehended.

———

It was my original intention, in accordance with my custom, to be brief in my relation of Chinese matters : but, to satisfy the curious, I shall place before them a representation of the mountains which in the course of this my journey I closely observed. I shall, however, first relate the reasons for my undertaking of this journey, and thereafter the graciousness and respect which the emperor constantly evinced towards us. The emperor, learning that for some years past we had accomplished the manufacture of certain pipes or tubes, of various qualities of clay, which sometimes, by the intervention of men, and sometimes even without such, gave out in answer to each other musical sounds, sought to learn the theory and manner of this invention, and when he was made to understand it, proceeded to utter exclamations of astonishment, and to extol this our so successful contrivance.

The emperor, being a wise and far-seeing man, intelligent and good natured, readily acknowledged that to this hour the contrivance in question had been unknown to the Chinese. It was his pleasure to pass the summer season about and among the mountains of Tartary, for the benefit of the air. He announced this decision to me in words to this effect. " Now that I have attentively examined the art of your music it greatly pleases me. Your wisdom delights me. You must become the companion of my journey, that I may have the enjoyment of your skill while I am hunting." He desired to have books of science and such like translated into Chinese, saying that his people would study them with special application.

Father Ferdinand Verbiest being present when the emperor made this communication, foreseeing the inconvenience which awaited me, particularly from the scarcity of cold water, of which, by reason of an illness, I required a large supply (the Chinese drink no water which is not warmed), and representing this difficulty to his majesty, the latter answered that everything necessary should be provided. We thanked him as became us. On the following day he commanded his uncle and his father-in-law that they should take us in charge with due honour, and that raiment should be supplied to me from the imperial wardrobe, a thing hitherto unknown. He perhaps mislikes our poverty, which contrasts so strongly with the splendour of his court. All these directions were forthwith carried into effect, so far as the shortness of the time allowed. And certainly this precaution was not useless, for the cold in these regions is that of our January. The emperor further directed, in evidence of his good will and esteem, that two horses should be supplied daily from his own stable for my use. I, meanwhile, thus equipped, betook myself in all haste at midnight to the hills, the emperor being accustomed to choose that season for travelling, so as to avoid the heat, and to take up his abode on the mountains near the great Wall, which separates Tartary from China. Since I have seen with my own eyes, to my great wonder, this Wall, which exceeds all others in length and breadth, some mention of it may not be unacceptable. It is a work of great excellence, which cost inconceivable labour, untold sums, and thousands of lives ; and yet it is useless as a fortification for defence or security, wherefore its authors at this day enjoy but a poor reputation. I would here go through its history from beginning to end, had it not been so repeatedly furnished by other writers; so that I could say nothing new on the subject, especially of the three hundred miles at which its length is reckoned, which may in fact be more correctly stated at nine hundred, if we count the sinuosities and the course of the rampart round and over precipices and projecting rocks, in the which haunt great serpents, but no other wild animal as far as I have seen. In the fields near this Wall tents or huts are raised, and in these we have to pass the nights; for the emperor is wont to encamp in these valleys and desert flats, near a river, that he may avoid becoming a burthen to the inhabitants and to the towns. When he thus halts for some days two tents are erected as palaces, the one for a dining-hall and for morning repose, the other for night repose: a very great work and perfect in all particulars, but composed of mats, yet worth some eight thousand ducats in value. The princes and grandees, on their part, are also very regularly lodged.

Admiration is excited when one considers the delicacies and fresh fruits which are conveyed hither from Pekin by divers messengers; and what care is taken meanwhile of the administration of justice, of which nothing is concealed from the emperor, but everything as well ordered as though he were present.

While these things were passing, the emperor was advised of an advantageous occurrence with the Russians touching a certain fortress, which, remaining in the hands of the latter, had been very prejudicial to the hunting and to the pearl fishery. There was much congratulation on the acquirement of this place, the more as it had occurred without much bloodshed. It gave occasion to the emperor to ask me many questions about the Russians.

On the third day, he called me to his presence that I might play him some music, in which art he takes special delight. I expounded it from its first elements, to the great satisfaction of all hearers, and to the utmost of my ability, and the emperor paid as much attention as if the fate of his empire were concerned; but when I had finished, his desires led him again to the chase.

On the fifth day we pursued our journey between mountains, which seemed to threaten us on either side. The precipices are fearful on account of the narrowness of the way, which, not without great cost and incomparable labour, has been so far improved, that not only access is afforded to the hunting grounds, but that many Chinese avail themselves of its facilities to establish themselves in the neighbourhood of the great wall; by which state policy the emperor not only extends his territory, but keeps at a respectful distance the Western Tartar tribes, who, were they strong enough, would act hostilely towards the Chinese. When the emperor goes beyond the frontier, it is incredible how much cavalry he takes with him. Towards evening the camp of the soldiery was pitched in a level field, watered by four rivers, which descend from the mountains. This part of Tartary consists of high hills, which are clothed with wood, and would be agreeable if we could deprive them of the rudeness of their precipices. Several races of people have established themselves in these districts by command of the emperor; and here dwell the Tartars, who are peculiarly addicted to the chase, building themselves huts, and enjoying a superfluity of wild animals, with the skins of which they clothe themselves. The soil here is very fertile, producing all kinds of grain. The forest superabounds in fruitbearing trees; pears, apricots, apples and peaches, are in plenty. These afford not only food for foxes, wild swine, and other animals, but also profit to many who pluck these fruits for nothing, and sell them again dear enough. There are also other fruits not known among us, which are sold at high prices to those who pursue the chase in these mountains.

When I was the companion of the emperor I followed his example in tasting these novel delicacies, and much relished them, especially some grapes of an extraordinary flavour. On account of the narrowness and steepness of the road, I dismounted and led my horse. The emperor and the princes of West Tartary in all this went on in advance, without regard to the danger. What I have said of these mountains may be understood as applicable to the others, unless we except those which extend themselves to the westward.

At this part of our journey we were obliged to halt some days, on account of the illness of a son of the emperor's by one of his queens, for whose carriage the road had been so carefully mended and also watered, that nothing more perfect could exist. It makes me ashamed to reflect how imperfect in comparison is my service to God the Lord of heaven and earth. When the patient's sickness had somewhat abated, the emperor returned from a visit which he had paid to him. On the 25th day we girded ourselves again to our task, and crossed several rivers, bridges having been first laid over them. Every one made a push for the passage, although not free from danger, inasmuch as it was not safe to pass the night on the mountain, where tigers constantly abound. The spot which it was our object to reach at the end of this day's jour ney was four miles further on, and the day was nearly occupied with these passages of the rivers. After these had been effected the bridges were removed. They were made of heavy timbers like masts of ships, such as the timber traders on these rivers float down to the capital at Pekin, and receive there very high payment for the same. I stood amazed to behold such enormous trees, springing out of the bare rock. We came finally to the appointed halting-place, near another great river, which descending southward, spreads itself out for a short space into a standing water. On account of the distance, we were obliged to supply the place of tents by other contrivances, for the encamping materials could not be brought on so far. For this reason the emperor is minded for another year to build residences, in places like this where he is accustomed to halt, on the spot, without regard to the cost. All the architects and artificers are therefore ordered from Pekin to assemble in this distant region. Were the emperor not master of such vast territory and wealth, such a work could not be accomplished. Six sumptuous pavilions were erected, the first for the sole use of the emperor, the other for the queens, according to their rank, and for the prince, the eldest son, a successor to the throne, all alike of lacquer-work with tin lining, seven or eight ells in height, so that no one from without could look in. The entrance, after the fashion of the Chinese, faced the south, being guarded from the weather by curtains of the most costly silk damask.

On either side stood two tents for the princes and councillors of state, who wait upon the emperor twice a day; there is also another place for those with whom he has more private intimacy, among whom I was included, having liberty to go in and out at my pleasure; but this great privilege I was careful not to make too free use of. It behoved me to be cautious and circumspect, in order to avoid incurring disfavour from others.

Round the tents which I have described as thus magnificent, were magazines, and beyond these a net was drawn, made of thick and heavy cordage, seven feet high, which supplies the place of a second wall. In this there was a back entrance to the north, and another entrance to the south, at which were stationed troops of the body guard, and further inwards was the quarter of the halberdiers. Without this circle was another, formed of tents, adjusted so close to one another as to leave no interval, in which the soldiers kept guard for our greater security day and night. About two bowshots from this were encamped the princes and nobility, so near each other as to make a fourth wall. The common

18

multitude lay without, in very good order, so that every one could without trouble find his own place. On each side of the river, for half a mile or a mile in extent, was a double row of tents, which served to secure the access on either bank to the stream. The princes of the West remained beyond this defence. The number of men was so great, that I should in vain attempt to state it, and am silent for fear of error and of contradicting other authorities. The emperor, being minded to devote the day to the chase, required a double supply of horses and camels, and those which were needed for this purpose of his majesty's use were so quickly furnished, that he found everything in readiness at the appointed spot with as little confusion as if there were nothing to do, from which it is easy to infer the abundance of pasturage in the meadows on the banks of the river, but for which the proceeding would have been impossible.

Moving forward from this place on the thirtieth day, we came incontinently upon another very rapid river, at which the emperor, out of regard for our safety, made proclamation that not more than two horsemen at a time should ride over the bridge, which protracted the passage till evening, and caused many to remain on the hither side.

Some days after the chase, when everyone had risen before daylight, the emperor went forward in advance of all, and everyone took his meal when he chose, the hour of dinner being uncertain ; and wheresoever half-cooked meat was served, of which these people are very fond, I was well content to get dry rice ; wherefore the emperor's father-in-law, when he invited me to his table, gave orders that I should be abundantly supplied with cold water and dry rice.

After the table was over, it was my daily habit to attend the court, and when the emperor mounted his horse, I followed among his principal nobles till sunset, without food, unless that be called such which the wild fruits afforded and which I enjoyed with moderation. This mode of life I maintained for three months. In the woods I met with edible mushrooms as large as our hats. When, for the purpose of the chase, the low country has been left and the mountain has been ascended, a circle is formed far and wide to enclose the wild beasts, in the manner as follows.

When the cavalry has been arranged under its respective standards, then, at a given signal, two horsemen with blue flags are sent forward, the one of whom gallops off to the right flank and the other to the left to a certain limit, so as in short time to reach the appointed spots, about two miles distance from each other. Elevated above the circle, which, at a signal given to the horsemen, is then formed, stands another long row of horsemen, who are thus placed the better to discover the beasts among the brushwood; in the middle of this position is planted the emperor's standard, a flag made of tin, which is usually carried before him as he rides at the head of a company. He made me the associate of this his so agreeable occupation, his notice being attracted to me, as I suppose, by the length of my beard, which was conspicuous among so many shaven chins; this took place in the midst of a plain full of quails, of which he shot some twenty with arrows before my eyes. The first mentioned circle of horsemen is succeeded by another, whose office it is to kill the animals which have slipped through the hands of the former. Between these first and last bands and the imperial standard, follows the entire train of courtiers on horseback, who are on the watch to catch the slightest sign of the emperor, so that among these rocks everything is at his hand the same as in the palace of Pekin. When the emperor moves to the higher ground, a fire is conveyed in an ingenious apparatus suspended between two horses, with a kettle containing Tartarian Cha or Tée, and warm water made from melted snow, with fresh fruits; and everything which can serve to excite the appetite is prepared with great expedition. At one time, when by accident a nest of tiger cubs had been discovered, some eunuchs in charge of the sheep loitered on their way, and occasioned the access to be left open. The culprit was immediately sentenced to walk on foot by the camels, which would have occasioned his death by fatigue, had not the emperor remitted the punishment; so heavy was the penalty ordained for so trifling an offence.

The last band is composed of the rabble, servants and attendants. The Western chieftains, as best accustomed to these forests, acted as commanders, allowing no one to leave his station. In the confined space the stags frequently put the riders in jeopardy, jumping six ells in distance. In these places are found the sweet mart (Martin cat), foxes, wolves, goats, sheep of various kinds, wild swine, roe deer, and other wild animals. Here also, as we have observed, are found tigers, against which the emperor is so incensed that he never spares them, but pursues them to the death; to which end he has proper weapons by him, and in particular two firelocks, which are always at hand. Wheresoever a river occurs abounding in fish, the chase is superseded, and all betake themselves to fishing; and for this purpose camels carry on their backs small boats made in separate pieces, which are put together and made available in an instant. When the parties come in sight of the tents the circle is contracted round the beasts gradually, sometimes with the addition of two bands of horsemen, with blue flags, which is done by special command of the emperor. I, who had no other purpose but to drive the game within shot of the emperor, have nevertheless caught an animal between my legs, which much pleased the emperor. Nor is it unfrequent that the wildest animals are thus easily captured, when the circle has once closed in upon them. The horsemen then dismount, and leave their horses outside the circle, that they may keep closer together and repulse the animals, which would otherwise escape between the legs of the horses.

When the slaughter is over, camels are laden with the bodies, and hastily driven to the emperor, and there sentence is given as in a court of justice how the skins shall be removed, and the meat cut up in pieces fit to be dried in the sun and preserved against corruption. Laden with these spoils everyone towards evening betook himself to his tent, and by the following morning all were again in readiness. When the emperor occasionally dismounted for awhile, I used to allow myself a little sleep, not with an eye open, like the Chinese, who, when on horseback, are easily overtaken by slumber, but so that they seem to be awake. It sometimes occurred, that when the emperor wished to show favour to some of his principal courtiers, he would cut some morsels of venison with his own hand from a stag's carcase for himself, and then would grant the same privilege to the favourites in question. Upon this each one would collect a bundle of faggots, and exhorted me to imitate their example, which, like another Diogenes, I performed, curious as to the purpose of the ceremony. And behold spits were produced, and large fires lighted, to which some held their portions of meat, others flung the pieces into the fire for a moment, and then swallowed them, still dripping with blood, with great relish. These were of the older mandarins, for the younger people born in China laughed at the proceeding, which I gazed at in silence and wonder. Some consider stag's flesh, with salt and vinegar, a great delicacy. The emperor looked on with satisfaction, as on a thing to which he was habituated. In the thickets of this country there are many varieties of potherbs, namely, white and red onions, which I conjecture to have been brought from Egypt, much basilicum, but wild, and other vegetables, of which the names were unknown to us. Persian roses are as abundant as thistles or brambles with us; cloves flourish in great quantity, with four leaves, but without perfume; and many other things, more than I could mention without prolixity, albeit truly recounted. Trees not bearing fruit abound, as with us, such as oaks, poplar, and beech, which cover the mountains.

Several small rivers run into that which we have noticed for its swiftness, and of these the water is very good and cold, which is ascribable to the vegetation which shadows their course and protects them from the heat of the sun.

On these mountains, which, according to concurrent opinion of all have never before our expedition been ascended by man, trees are sometimes observed which have been injured by fire, a spectacle which greatly puzzled me when I beheld it. The Chinese will have it that these trees have been set on fire, like tinder, by the mere rays of the sun; which I could myself credit, were it not that the fact occurs often in the instance of green wood as well as of that which has gone to decay. Nor does this theory agree with other features of the case, for I have seen these trees marked with fire on the north side, as well as on that which is exposed to the southern sun. Many are also found thus consumed in hollows and recesses, which the sun never penetrates; many also are burnt at bottom and still green at top; others are entirely burnt in the stems, while the leaves are still flourishing. I have myself remarked, that this conflagration always begins from the stems, which are certainly less exposed to the sun than the branches.

The Chinese, convinced by the above and such like arguments, questioned me warmly as to my opinion of the cause of these fires. I made them, to the best of my ability, understand that the sun could not be the cause; it is known to all that the chase is continually pursued in these mountains, especially that of the stag, an animal which sheds its horns annually, and at this season is so plagued by the continual itching, that he rubs his horns to and fro with great violence against any substance, till he gets rid of the itching and the horns together. For this purpose the stems serve him, and he rubs against them till the friction produces fire, and thus

the stems are easily destroyed, especially in the case of pine
trees, which, even when flourishing, supply ready fuel for
the flames. This explanation satisfied the Chinese. Rotten
wood gives out a light of itself by night, so strong that the
smallest writing may be read by it.

It was the emperor's pleasure that I should explain to him
the cause of this light, which I was able to do to the satisfaction and agreement of his majesty.

By these and such like questions I was kept in continual
occupation, but my answers obtained great applause and consideration.

One of the great men of the court said to me, " If we
Tartars were to choose another religion than our own, I
should embrace your's, because I never put anything
before its teachers but that I receive satisfaction in reply ;"
it is for this reason no one contradicts us, for fear of being
laughed at by the bystanders, which coming to the ears of
the emperor, made him say in joke to his courtiers, " Take
heed of controversy with the Christian teachers, for their
knowledge compels you to agree with them on every subject,
and, what is more, they worship in my presence, when occasion offers, the highest God." Many of the courtiers, who
used formerly to address their prayers to heaven, are now
ashamed to use that name, and only pray to the personal
God.

I would wish also to mention the care and order which
they observe without intermission on their march. No one
strays, either to the right or to the left, and whensoever the
difficulty of the road compels them to dismount, each man
leads his horse by the bridle and preserves his rank ; and
even under heavy rain no one leaves the road to take shelter
under the trees, but only wraps himself in a waterproof
garment.

On the 9th of August we reached the mountain Pe Cha,
the appointed termination of our journey. This spot, towards

which one continually ascends, is, according to the observations of fathers Ferdinand Verbiest and Philip Grimaldi, a
full mile in height. It was so cold here that ten thousand
horses died on the night of our arrival; the which were not
even missed, whence may be inferred the prodigious number
of horses in our company.

This mountain, which in most parts is smooth in surface,
is about three miles in extent, and in the more rugged
parts is covered with wood; but the streams consist rather
of mud than of water, which was very unsuitable for our
horses.

In the middle is a lake, said to be unfathomable, but which
may rather be said to resist the attempt to fathom it, being
always frozen. The emperor's father-in-law speaking much
of it, persuaded me to visit it.

Many rivers, which ultimately water different quarters of
the world, have their sources in this mountain. The earth
is hard frozen throughout the year, except in the dog days,
when it is thawed to the depth of two ells. The consequence
is that the fir trees, contrary to their nature, pushing their
roots only to this depth, are often in masses of great extent
levelled to the ground by the high winds, where otherwise
they would only perish by slow decay. When the emperor
asked me how I was pleased with these great mountains, I
replied, that nothing could gratify me more than their distant aspect, covered as they were with a mantle of wood,
green and thick as standing corn, a spectacle with which
the eye is never satiated; this answer much pleased him,
as it quite coincided with his own feeling. About this time
many petty sovereigns came to pay their respects to the emperor, whom he received with much courtesy. There came
also certain La Ma, a sort of bonzes, who say that they are
originally from Thibet. These bonzes are in great reputation, so that they attain to positions of the highest honour;
but their god is their belly. They worship the false god Fo.

If their law be examined, it is found to forbid them to eat flesh; but these men, who were among the most considerable of their body, avowed openly that they devoured flesh even uncooked and raw; and when I flung this in reproach against them, asking who were the real bonzes, they replied that the real bonzes were fools, and that they laughed at them. In the summer season they go with arms, shoulders, and breast uncovered, but in autumn they cover themselves with the most costly furs, except with some of a particular pale colour, the use of which is confined to the emperor.

The cold being very severe on this mountain, we moved from Pe-Cha on the fifth day after the imperial tents had been pitched. We saw vast numbers of people, who were employing in drying the flesh and hides of the dead horses for future consumption on the journey. They will eat also mules and other quadrupeds, salting the hides and devouring the flesh with voracity.

On our return journey the camp was divided into two wings, the one of which escorted the queens on the road by which they had come, the other attended the emperor towards the east, in order to follow the chase of certain animals, called in Chinese Hoam Yam. This name is applied both to sheep and goats, without any difference in the sound. In the horns this animal has some resemblance to the goat, but has no beard. It is black in colour, and so active in its spring that you might swear that it flies. One of them, after losing one of its legs, I saw, with my own eyes, distance a swift horse which was spurred to the utmost in pursuit.

The day came to an end in the emperor's chase of this animal without success, for it escaped before our approach; the emperor in consequence passed the night in pursuit of hares and rabbits (called, without distinction between the two, Teao Tu), animals which, from fear of man, conceal themselves during the day in holes and nests, but when the sun goes down take to the meadows. These rabbits have

19

very long hinder legs and fore legs of scarce a finger's length, so that they can only move by jumps. In other respects they resemble ours, but have longer tails.

Of this particular chase I shall say no more, as it differed in nothing remarkable from the others before mentioned, except that all pursued it on foot, not excepting the emperor, who comported himself like one of the common train, and thus was the night passed in this chase by moonlight; and when the latter failed, torches were lighted. The European rabbit is unknown in all China, except the domestic variety, which is of divers colours. Here is abundance of hares, which the Tartars do not eat, but the Chinese do very greedily; as they also do mice, cats, and dogs. This western district is a vast plain, sandy in its soil, and abounding in sheep.

On the 29th of August we fell in with a flock of sheep, a sign of the proceedings of a company which the emperor had ordered on in advance, with the intent of killing the sheep by night, which was effected. These animals are altogether wild, and never check their flight till they are beyond sight of the hunter.

On this occasion the emperor was unwearied as another Hercules, killing, out of a second flock, mostly with his own spear, a thousand sheep. In these two flocks were captured two wolves, which kept company with the old sheep and fed on the young.

This chase being concluded we moved on, first to the north and then to the south, very desirous to fall in again with another flock, which had escaped us in the Pe Cha mountain. This we accomplished on the 8th of September, at a place where a river flows out of the mountain; and here lodges had been erected, according to orders of the emperor, for himself and others. When we had rested here some days the camp was again divided, one part following the march of the queens towards Pekin, the other attending the emperor towards the north-east, with the purpose of laying a new ambush against the stags, who for some months together make such a belling that the females hearing it resort to them, and their male rivals also seek an encounter. The consequence is, that running with great speed they fall into the hands of the hunters, which gave great contentment to the emperor. But this contentment lasted not long ; for on the 16th and 17th of September fell a heavy snow, a not unusual circumstance for the season in this district, and threatened us with a failure of provision ; which placed the emperor in great straights, and caused him to depart in haste towards Pekin. Before his departure, however, it pleased him to distribute among his great men the overplus of the spoil which had accumulated during his three months' hunting. I, unworthy as I was of such honour, received my share among the first, for which I made my humble acknowledgments, after the Chinese fashion.

Early on the morning of the 28th September the emperor, receiving accounts of the illness of his grandmother, pursued his way with all speed towards Pekin, and with him many of his court, the others following more slowly with the queens. Although the emperor, with excessive regard to my convenience, desired that I should be spared the fatigue of attending him, I considered myself, in return for his kindness, the more obliged to follow him. And thus, travelling day and night for fifty miles, I reached a resting-place, so wearied that I could not bend a joint in my body. The labour, however great, had, as our experience showed, its reward ; not only in an increase of the emperor's favour, but in the friendship, thus acquired, of many great men, with whom, but for this opportunity, we could have contracted no acquaintance. They discover that we are masters of all sciences, and question us on every subject.

Of the journeys which the emperor sometimes makes in Tartary, the Jesuit Le Compte speaks as follows. " He goes often into Tartary to take the diversion of the chase, but always accompanied as though he were going to the conquest of another empire. He takes with him not less than 40,000 men, who sometimes suffer much, whether the season be hot or cold ; for he encamps in an inconvenient manner, and it often occurs that in a day of these laborious expeditions, more horses perish than in a stricken battle. He reckons, however, as nothing the loss of 10,000 horses. The fathers who have accompanied him aver, that his magnificence never appears more conspicuous on any other occasion. He receives sometimes twenty or thirty subordinate kings of the Tartar tribes, who come to make their court to him or to pay him tribute ; among them are even found some entitled to the name of *ham* or *kam*, which signifies emperor. They are all his pensionaries, on the footing of mandarins of the first order. He gives them his daughters in marriage, and in order to attach them more closely, he declares himself their protector against the Western Tartars, who often give him trouble, and who are even strong enough occasionally to attack China with success. While this crowd of petty sovereigns is in the camp, the court is most sumptuous ; and in order to impress these barbarians with an idea of the power of China, the train, the attire, and the tents of the mandarins, are rich to profusion and excess."

INDEX.

LONDON:
T. RICHARDS, 37, GREAT QUEEN STREET

For EU product safety concerns, contact us at Calle de José Abascal, 56–1°, 28003 Madrid, Spain or eugpsr@cambridge.org.